Writing in America

Writing in America

Edited by John Fischer and Robert B. Silvers

RUTGERS UNIVERSITY PRESS

NEW BRUNSWICK, CAMDEN, AND NEWARK,

NEW JERSEY, AND LONDON

Library of Congress Cataloging in Publication Number: 2017054965

A British Cataloging-in-Publication record for this book is available from the British Library.

∞ The paper used in this publication meets the requirements of the American National Standard for Information Sciences—Permanence of Paper for Printed Library Materials, ANSI Z39.48-1992.

www.rutgersuniversitypress.org

Manufactured in the United States of America

Contents

Most of the material contained in this volume previously appeared in a special supplement to the October, 1959, issue of *Harper's Magazine*.

Writing in America

CHAPTER I

The Wider and Wiser Use of Books

MASON W. GROSS

The National Book Committee has invited me to say something about the wider and wiser use of books. Inevitably that entails discussing books and authors, and equally unescapably reading and writing. The points I hope to make in these connections are not all of them polite or politic. Obviously, no teacher like myself can quarrel with the notion of the wider use of books, since that is a notion I try to pound into the heads of my students every day. But that word "wiser" is calculated to make any philosopher's hackles rise. Admittedly, it is indeed a wonderful thing to write a book and have it published, and I speak in no spirit of personal sour grapes. If some of the remarks which follow on the matter of wisdom appear harsh, they are not so intended, but the issue of wisdom was raised by the Committee and is of its choosing.

Years ago I received a gentle but firm rebuke from one of my philosophy teachers at Harvard, the late Professor David Wright Prall, whose departmental specialty was esthetics. I had been expressing some rather caustic comments on a late nineteenth-century symphony, a work which I did not consider altogether up to par. Professor Prall would have none of my superciliousness. He pointed out to me what an incredible thing it was to be able to compose a symphony

_____

A speech before the National Book Committee in New York on November 18, 1959.

at all, let alone one which could measure up to the lofty standards of a Harvard Graduate student. So, remembering that gentle rebuke today, I should be sorry to convey the impression that I think that either writing or publishing is easy.

Reading is not always easy either, especially reading wisely. First of all reading wisely is obviously to be able to select and read only good books, and to leave the bad ones aside. Perhaps it is boorish in this company to suggest that there are any bad books—instead I should refer to good books, and less good ones, bearing in mind the contention of Saint Augustine that evil is only the absence of good. I assume, however, that we can get general agreement that some books are much better than others, and that some indeed are really good. Now my question is: What criterion or criteria are we using today to determine which are the really good books, the books which the wise reader, after wide reading, will select for his private edification? The wise man presumably does not read only for pleasure, although real pleasure may accompany all his reading. There is some other quality, or it may be some combination of qualities, which provides the main source of attraction.

I ask this question from several points of view. As chairman of the Rutgers University Press Council, I am involved in decisions as to whether to publish this or that new title. As a teacher I am required to recommend readings for my students. As a reader I have for over thirty years devoured the book reviews in the newspapers and the literary magazines. And as a booklover whose available income has not gone up as rapidly as the price of books, I have in the bookstores painful decisions to make. In all these capacities I feel vaguely uneasy. I would like to publish, to buy, and to assign only books of whose excellence I had reason to be assured; and perhaps it is only advancing age and squeamishness that make me uneasy. But somehow I have the feeling that while there are lots of relatively good books, there are very few whose excellence is so compelling that I must not delay before getting down to my reading. I shall be bold enough to confess that all too often I manage to convince myself that a given title will either be remaindered for 59 cents, or will be republished in paperback form before long, and that I can easily wait for that. This may be heresy, but I have to confess to it.

Since we are all interested in books, I think that perhaps I should try to describe what I miss in so much of our contemporary literature, and why these days I feel a diminished urge to go out and buy a book I have just heard about. What I believe I miss is the conviction that the author has something of such great importance to say to me that I cannot afford to be without whatever it is that he is saying. In other words, I suspect that the author is not really trying to persuade me of anything. He probably has something to say, which has to some degree prompted his writing the book. But I somehow do not get an assurance that he is really trying to persuade me of anything, and therefore I do not feel any specially personal reason why I should suddenly join his reading public. He probably has written a good book—the reviewers tell me so. It would probably enlighten me to read it—the blurbs tell me so. I am probably wrong in not reading it at once—the book clubs tell me so. But still, the impression that I am sufficiently important to the writer that he has taken the trouble to try to convince me personally of something, simply is not there. And I should add that when subsequently I do get around to spending my 59 cents, the impression does not leave me. In short, because I do not feel that I am important to the author, I, perhaps arrogantly, infer that he is not important to me.

There used to be taught in our schools and colleges a subject known as the art of persuasion, or rhetoric. Its textbook was Aristotle's *Rhetoric,* or Cicero's *De Oratore,* or Quintilian, and its materials included Demosthenes, Bossuet and Lincoln. A fascinating course can still be built around these materials, but there will be few takers. The college debate has replaced persuasion, and the art of rhetoric has been supplanted by public speaking—"You Too Can Talk Well."

Now I suggest that what is wrong with our authors today—with all too few exceptions—is that they are insufficiently schooled in the art of persuasion. I would like to suggest further some things about this art of persuasion which I find wanting in too much of our contemporary prose.

In the first place the rhetoricians were fascinated to an incredible degree by words—just words. No musician was ever more entranced by subtle variations in sound, no painter was ever more in love with his pigments and what he could make them do, than was Cicero in his devotion to words. I suggest that nowadays most of us don't even know what it is to be in love with words. That is perhaps a pastime for poets, or a joke for people like Gertrude Stein, or a disease for people like Thomas Wolfe. Some of our contemporary public speakers seem to love certain oral sounds and give them the full treatment; others have a passion, it would seem, for certain verbal formulae, usually clichés; still others just love the sound of their own voices. None of these know what it is to be in love with words and entranced with their magic. We have, of course, our E. B. White and J. D. Salinger, and a few others, but then we never hesitate to rush out and buy *their* books.

But words, their meanings, their combinations, their sounds and their rhythms, are only the beginning. The second concern of the rhetorician was with the intellectual equipment of his would-be orator, or his author. Here it astonishes contemporary readers to learn that a Cicero or a Quintilian will draw no limits as to what his pupils should come to know. The present-day public speaker, and too many authors, are expected to achieve mastery only of the subject concerning which they are presently giving utterance—all other intellectual resources are for the moment irrelevant. And so we tend to pass up their books and wait for the next volume by Sir Winston Churchill, whose fare is always rich.

Most of all, however, the rhetorician never forgot that his job was to be persuasive, and that that meant always keeping an audience in mind. First of all you had to know who the audience was to be, and then you had to learn all that could be learned about that audience—its moral standards, its habits of behavior, its psychological make-up, and its probable attitudes towards the subject under discussion. There is no doubt in my mind that the chief reason that so many of the great classics seem to speak so directly to us is that the authors were consciously trying to reach us, or at least people with an astonishing resemblance to us. For me it is almost embarrassing to read Stendhal—he seems to know me so well. And Fielding always seems anxious to introduce me to people whom he is sure I will like. Hume gives me the impression that he has turned a phrase for my particular delectation, and Descartes obviously is trying to win me over. This gift of reaching me personally is surely the author's greatest gift, but I am confident that it comes only as the result of serious intent.

All these, however, are still subordinate to the main objective of rhetoric, which is to persuade people *of something.* Ever since the time of Plato we have been suspicious of the very word rhetoric, or Plato's synonym for it, sophistry. Sure we know all about the fascination of words, and the all-too-ready erudition of the speaker with a smooth, glib tongue, and a gift of seducing the unwary hearer. Plato felt, and he expressed his belief so cogently that we have all been persuaded since, that the art of persuasion was inimical to the discovery of absolute truth. Rhetoric might be all right for lawyers who get paid for winning cases, or for preachers who may have to frighten reluctant souls into salvation, but essentially it was opposed to the true work of the intellect.

Now Plato can never be ignored. His own skill in persuasion is so great that he carries us along with him in his war against the art of persuasion—which of course any great orator should be able to do. But before we think that we are Platonists in our suspicion concerning rhetoric, it would be well for us to examine the structure of a number of Plato's dialogues. Consider the *Euthyphro,* where we are seeking a definition of piety and holiness, or the first book of the *Republic* where the topic is a definition of justice, or the *Symposium* and its discussion concerning love. There is a progression in each of these dialogues which is designed to bring us closer and closer to a final understanding of the topic in question. The second step in this progression is usually the introduction of a sophist or a sophistical treatment of the subject. But this is only the second step—Thrasymachus in the *Republic* or Pausanias in the *Symposium*. I would like to draw your attention to the first step–what I may call the pre-sophistical or pre-rhetorical step. Here we find a Euthyphro or a Phaedrus or a Polemarchus. And who are these people? You know them only too well. They are the well-born, well-educated, knowledgeable, articulate and serious-minded young men, who are well-drilled in the clichés of their day. Their sentences parse; their historical examples and their mythological references can be checked against the Book of Knowledge; their intent is somber and humor-less, but pure and serene. They have done no real thinking for them-selves but they pass for thinking men because they are so serious. Athens was full of them, and so is New York. Some of them are probably sitting in our publishing houses right now, with neatly typed manuscripts waiting patiently in shiny leather briefcases. They have nothing to say to you or me, but they say it most acceptably.

Remember that Plato quietly demolishes these people before he permits his sophists to come rushing in like bulls. The trivialities have to be cleared out of the way before we can get down to the war of ideas, where Plato's absolutes come to grips with relational modes of thinking. Nowadays few of us are able to follow Plato to his ultimate conclusion, but unless we can follow him, we will have to re-evaluate his devastating criticism of the rhetoricians.

What we must remember is that when Plato introduced a soph-ist he also began to discuss an idea, an idea which both he and the sophist considered very important indeed. His bright young men had no ideas—they were not trying to persuade anybody of any-thing. They were just part of the cultural scene. But the sophists were excited about ideas and were trying to persuade people that they were right. And Plato was excited about ideas and was trying to use non-rhetorical methods of persuasion. I venture to suggest that before we join Plato in his attack on the relativism of the Sophists, we ask ourselves whether we have in fact got as far as chapter two in a Platonic dialogue, or whether possibly we are not still in chapter one, where everyone goes through all the right motions, but where ideas are really not worth fighting about.

This, then, is surely the important point. If the art of persuasion is to come into its own again we must first have something to persuade people of. We must have ideas which are desperately important, and we must be desperately concerned to convince a concretely envisaged audience of their importance. Then we must study our audience—how do we get through to them? What are they like? What will appeal to them and stir them into action or strong feeling? Next we must consider ourselves; by what right do we take this issue to them? Do we know what we are talking about? Do we speak from a firm base of knowledge and wide experience? Are we truly educated in the matters relevant to the issue in question? Or are we biassed peddlers of a narrow and prejudiced point of view? And then, if we can satisfactorily answer the other questions, we may ask ourselves if we have the necessary tools to carry out the job of persuasion. The point here is that unless we feel a burning desire to say something because we believe it is important, we will never persuade ourselves to take the trouble to say it in the most persuasive manner possible. And if we do not say it persuasively, we have no reason to blame the reading public if it does not take it or us seriously.

We hear comment on all sides about the decline and fall of the English language. We are told that high school graduates can neither read nor write, and that college graduates aren't much better. We work up a furious head of puristic steam because somebody says that a certain cigarette tastes good like a cigarette should. Nobody can spell any more; no one knows what it means to parse a sentence; nobody cares about the right meanings of words. So run the lamentations.

I can easily join this chorus myself. I remember a sticker which the State of New Jersey required me and all my fellow automobile owners in New Jersey to keep on my windshield for six months and which said on the back in large block letters, "Safety and courtesy are synonymous." I have found no one yet who wrote to the State Department of Motor Vehicles to object to being required to propagate this falsehood. I recently received an invitation to give a baccalaureate address. It was explained in the letter that although the exercise would be held on a Sunday, it was not a religious service, and that it would not be necessary for me to make any "bibliographical" references. And so it goes. The obvious answer always is: Oh, well, you know what I mean. But a man never says: Oh, well, you know what I mean, if he is trying to persuade you of something. And so I come back to my original point, which is that what I miss in contemporary literature and the contemporary use of the English language is the sense that some one is trying to persuade me of something—something so important that he simply has to enlist me in his cause.

And this is a horrible thought. Never in all history has there been a time of more crucial importance for humanity, never a time when it was more important to enlist the full intellectual powers of man to cope with problems which threaten his very existence as a species. And what do we find ourselves doing? We are mouthing stale clichés, meaningless formulae, tired platitudes. Where new ideas must be found, we come up with verbal jingles which we do not take seriously.

Obviously what is needed, and needed desperately today, is a whole new flood of ideas—ideas firmly believed, and ideas eloquently expressed. We need ideas about how to live with the Russians, and ideas about how to live with the Chinese. We need ideas about how to improve the quality of our national performance abroad. We need ideas about how to solve our domestic problems at home. I cannot believe that the American people have yet gone bankrupt so far as ideas are concerned. What we seem to lack is the atmosphere which encourages strange and new ideas.

There are several places where we could hope that this atmosphere would develop. One place would be on the campuses of our universities. Of late the atmosphere on university campuses has been marked by a cautiousness and conservatism. There is probably less student political activity now than at any period in the history of American colleges. The period that we have recently gone through; the constant investigations as to what one did and said when one was an undergraduate twenty or thirty years ago; the feeling that this is not the time to stick your neck out—all these have meant that the atmosphere has not vibrated with new ideas, controversies, and concern over our national and international future. To be sure, fewer people are punished nowadays for saying things that are out of line. But I am afraid that the principal reason for that is that nobody is saying anything out of line, and therefore there is no occasion for punishment.

Another place where we can hope to encourage an atmosphere that is receptive to new ideas is in the whole realm of the printed word—whether this be books, magazines, or newspapers. But here again instead of finding much of an outlet for fiery discussions of new and startling ideas, we find a constant and continual rehash of the old and familiar ones. And precisely because they are old and familiar, because they don't carry with them the aura of immediate conviction, they are usually expressed in shoddy and weary language.

We have had a curious experience recently in New Jersey, one of limited significance but possibly of considerable interest. We have been conducting a campaign to persuade the voters to approve the issuance of bonds to the extent of $66,000,000 for new construction at the State University and the six State Colleges, and the Newark College of Engineering. Never in my life have I seen such an enthusiastic response on behalf of all the students, the faculty, the alumni, and friends of the various colleges. Here was a crusade that they could go for without any question whatsoever. Meeting after meeting was well attended. Time after time the speaker was cheered for his eloquence, and I am happy to report that the bond issue passed with a very comfortable margin in spite of significant opposition.

The point is that here was a crusade; here was something that people could do; here was a place for using the art of persuasion; and the response was tremendous. I can't help feeling that an immense flood of energy that had been bottled up so far as even more significant causes are concerned, was let loose on this particular campaign, and people had a wonderful time in so doing. If only this same energy could be let loose on topics of vaster importance there is a possibility that this might have astonishing consequences. Apathy might suddenly yield to a tremendous burst of interest and enthusiasm. Whether our New Jersey illustration is valid or not, it still seems to me to be clear that until we re-establish persuasion on significant issues as the central objective of our most of our publications, we will not have any vigorous interchange of ideas, we will not have any brilliantly clear prose, we will not have any strong feeling that we must go out and read this book at once. Once we find people trying to persuade us of something, then Ave can go on to chapter three in Plato and try to learn from him our way through the various techniques of persuasion to the discovery of the truth. But nobody ever discovered the truth who was bored by the whole idea, or felt that the truth could be conveyed by any casual and dull repetition of clichés. Currently I feel that as educators and as bookmen, we are playing everything altogether too safe. We don't want to rock the boat. We don't want to upset the apple-cart. We don't want to stir things up in these difficult times.

Possibly what I am saying is that I would like to substitute articulate and open persuaders for the hidden persuaders who, we are told, influence so many of our current decisions. Rational discussion, rational argument, and eloquent persuasion can be our only substitute for these hidden and subtle forms of persuasion. We must get things out in the open and discuss them rationally and with conviction.

As we seek to promote the wider and wiser use of books, we can take as one criterion of the excellence of a book its attempt to persuade us of the importance of a new idea. The attempt may fail; the idea may be no good; but still we will not have wasted our time. If we are prepared to test our own clichés against a new idea, we can convert these clichés into strong positive restatements of ideas which still have validity and force for us. But the very fact that we have had to measure them against new ideas, and that we have had to withstand eloquent persuasion, will in itself be a remarkable way of sharpening our own mental powers. And with the attempt to persuade each other of the validity of our own ideas, we will recapture the art of persuasion, the art of eloquence, with all its devotion to clear and forceful expression and to the more sensitive and subtle use of language. At present language suffers because nobody is trying to say anything. When persuasion returns to the scene we will find our use of English becoming much sharper and much more pungent almost at once. Until this vitality returns to the world of books, there will continue to be no particular reason why we should explore contemporary literature in the hope of finding the kind of intellectual excitement that makes reading worthwhile.

We hope to persuade people to the wider and wiser use of books. If we are currently failing to persuade them it is because our authors are failing to persuade their readers of the importance and significance of whatever they say in their books. To be successful in this campaign therefore, we must try to recapture in our new books that sense of excitement which comes when somebody who believes something deeply and sincerely is trying with all the eloquence at his command to convert the particular audience that he has in mind. He needs to be unafraid to speak out, to speak clearly and plainly, to advocate what he believes. I am beginning to think that a cold war is not only a war in which there seems to be a disposition to fight but no actual fighting is going on, but also a war in which there is very little battling of ideas. The very presence of danger seems to have frightened us into silence, and from silence we drift into apathy. Books can arouse us from this apathy. In fact, it is one of their principal missions to do so. In this way may lie our national salvation.

CHAPTER 2

The Alone Generation

A Comment on the Fiction of the Fifties

ALFRED KAZIN

The other day a prominent American publisher advertised a book of stories by a Continental writer who died some time ago: "These stories, never before published in English, could only have been written by a great writer who flourished before World War II. They are stamped by that unobtrusive assurance, perfect sympathy with their subjects, and resonant tone which have become, it would seem, lost secrets in almost all the fiction of the immediate present." Not very encouraging, what? Yet I must admit that while I see a host of brilliantly talented writers all around me, I don't often get a very profound satisfaction out of the novels they write.

I am tired of reading for compassion instead of pleasure. In novel after novel, I am presented with people who are so soft, so wheedling, so importunate, that the actions in which they are involved are too indecisive to be interesting or to develop those implications which are the life-blood of narrative. The age of "psychological man," of the herd of aloners, has finally proved the truth of Tocqueville's observation that in modern times the average man is absorbed in a very puny object, himself, to the point of satiety. The whole interest of the reader seems to be summoned toward "understanding" and tolerance of the leading characters. We get an imaginative universe limited to the self and its detractors. The old-fashioned novel of sensitive souls, say Somerset Maugham's *Of Human Bondage* or even Sinclair Lewis's *Main Street,* showed a vulnerable hero or heroine battling it out (a) for principles which he identified with himself and (b) against social enemies who were honestly opposed to the protagonist's demand of unlimited freedom. Now we get novels in which society is merely a backdrop to the aloneness of the hero. People are not shown in actions that would at least get us to see the conditions of their personal struggle. Carson McCullers's beautiful first novel, *The Heart Is a Lonely Hunter,* characterized a stagnant society in the silent relationship between two mutes; in her third novel, *The Member of the Wedding,* the adolescent loneliness of Frankie fills up the scene, becomes the undramatic interest of the book, to the point where the reader feels not that he is witnessing a drama but that he is being asked to respond to a situation.

American society is remarkable for the degree of loneliness (not solitude) in which the individual can find himself. In our mass age, the individual's lack of privacy, his unlimited demand for self-satisfaction, his primary concern with his own health and well-being have actually thrown him back on himself more than before. Our culture is stupefyingly without support from tradition, and has become both secular and progressive in its articulation of every discontent and ambition; the individual now questions himself constantly because his own progress—measured in terms of the social norms—is his fundamental interest. The kind of person who in the nineteenth-century novel was a "character" now regards himself in twentieth-century novels as a problem; the novel becomes not a series of actions which he initiates because of *who* he is, but a series of disclosures, as at a psychoanalyst's, designed to afford him the knowledge that may heal him. It is astonishing how many novels concerned with homosexuality, on the order of Truman Capote's *Other Voices, Other Rooms,* are apologies for abnormality, designed to make us sympathize with the twig as it is bent the wrong way.

I would suspect that it is the intention of extracting "understanding" that accounts for the extraordinary number of children and adolescents in American fiction; at least in the imaginative society of fiction they can always be objects of concern. Even in a good writer like Capote, to say nothing of a bad writer like Gore Vidal, the movement of the book comes to a standstill in the grinding machinery of sensibility. As in James Baldwin's *Giovanni's Room,* sympathetic justice is always accorded homosexuals. No Vautrin as in Balzac, no Charlus as in Proust, no honest homosexual villains! The immediate result is the immobilization of narrative, the fashionable mistiness of prose; first the hero is cherished to the point of suffocation, then the style. *Other Voices, Other Rooms* is a brilliant effort of will, but it is unmoving rather than slow, retrospective rather than searching. In the past, the movement of fiction was more energetic than life; now fiction becomes vaguer, dimmer, an "exercise" in "craft."

This demand on our compassion is not limited to the quivering novels of sensibility by over-conscious stylists; it is the very essence of the deliberately churned-up novels of the Beat Generation. I mention Jack Kerouac here only because his novels, in which he has increasingly developed the trick of impersonating spontaneity by bombarding the reader with a mass of deliberately confused impressions, depend on a naked and unashamed plea for "love," understanding, fellowship, and are read and enjoyed only because this pleading so answers to our psychological interest in fiction that we indulge Kerouac without knowing why we do. Nothing human is now alien to us; after all, the fellow's problem could be our problem! It is ridiculous that novels can now be sent off as quickly as they are written and published immediately afterwards in order to satisfy the hopped-up taste of people who, when they open a novel, want to feel that they are not missing a thing. The sluttishness of a society whose mass ideal seems to be unlimited consumption of all possible goods and services is the reason for the "success" of writers whose literary strategy is to paint America as an unlimited supply of sex, travel, liquor, and lonely yearners. The individual who is concerned entirely with his aloneness will inevitably try to invade society, "the other" in his universe, by writing stormily, angrily, lashing the reader with a froth of words. But we are at fault in allowing the addict quality of such books to stand for "intensity" in fiction. More and more we judge novels by their emotional authenticity, not their creative achievement; we read them as the individual testifying for himself in a confused and troubling time. But the testimony is so self-concerned that we equate this glibness of feeling with reckless-ness of style. And here I come to another complaint, the increasing slovenliness, carelessness, and plain cowardice of style in fiction today.

We were wrong when we thought that the ghost of Henry James had put his too, too careful hand on our young 'uns. It is true that some of the new professor-novelists, Benjamin DeMott in *The Body's Cage* or Monroe Engel in *The Visions of Nicholas Solon,* like Capote himself in his first book and his stories, can remind us of the rage of style in the fiction of the forties. So talented a writer as Jean Staf-ford has of late years often seemed to bury herself in fine phrases. It is a rare professor-novelist, Robie Macauley in *The Disguises of Love,* who can escape the ostentatious carefulness, the jogging of the reader: *Please don't lose sight of my arm as I put together this beauti-ful edifice of words.* But actually, the increasing fussiness of our social ideals and the plain boredom of a period in which writers so often feel incapable of imagining decisive roles for their characters have led to the opposite quality. John Wain recently wrote:

"At the moment, the literary mind of the West seems to be swamped in one of its periodic waves of what George Orwell once called 'sluttish antinomianism,' which he defined as 'lying in bed drinking Pernod'."

What we get now is not the style of pretended fineness—the *New Yorker* ladies with every tuck in place—but the imitation of anger, the leer of the desperado. You can't fool us with your genteel learning, we're young American men who have been around and who have a punch! So I read in an article on fiction, by Herbert Gold, that something-or-other is like kissing a girl with spinach on her teeth. Wow, bang, and slam. Kerouac and whoever it is who follows *him* are "wild" in the hope of getting out of themselves, in finding some person, thing, or cause to latch onto. Gold is slovenly in the hope of sounding "cool"; he is understandably alarmed by the softness that threatens young novelists in so self-pitying an age as this. In England the young men are angry because they are still made to feel inferior; in America, young novelists get angry because they hope to sound belligerent and positive, *alive,* against the doldrums of the Eisenhower age.

One root of their difficulty is the irresistible example of Saul Bellow's *The Adventures of Augie March.* Anyone who has read his first two novels, *Dangling Man* and *The Victim,* knows that Bellow began with an almost excessive nobility of style, that the open and comically pretentious style in which Augie talks is a *tour de force.* Bellow has always been fascinated by characters who, in the deep Existentialist sense, are conscious of being *de trop,* excessive of themselves and their society, insatiable in their demands on life. All his representative men, in the phrase of Henderson the rain king, cry, *"I want! I want!"* This excess of human possibility over social goals, of the problem, man, over his intended satisfactions, led to a prose in *Augie* which is rapturously, not whiningly, faithful to all the signs and opportunities of experience. "If you've seen a winter London open thundering mouth in its awful last minutes of river light or have come with cold clanks from the Alps into Torino in December white steam then you've known like greatness of place." In *Augie,* Bellow attained a rosy deliverance from the grip of his past, he discovered himself equal to the excitement of the American experience, he shook himself all over and let himself go. "I am an American, Chicago born—Chicago, that somber city—and go at things as I have taught myself, free-style, and will make the record in my own way. . . ."

But just as no poet should attempt free verse who has not performed in traditional forms and meters, so no novelist should identify toughness with "free-style":

He brought his hand with the horny nail of his index finger in a wide circle, swinging an invisible lassoo, looping their belly-eyed gaze and taking it at his eye. They were caught first at the spongy wart on his nose and then in his eyes, working it for themselves now like the flies caught wriggling in sticky-paper. That wart made a stiff

flop when he tossed his head in beckon and hitch toward the
pungent foot-darkened sawdust at the door of Grack's Zoo, a gob-
ble of cajolery up from his throat and the swollen Adam's apple.

This is from Gold's most admired book, *The Man Who Was Not
With It,* and makes me think of what was once scrawled on a student paper at Harvard by ancient Dean Briggs: "falsely robust." I
think I understand where such worked-up militancy of phrase
comes from: from the novelist's honest need, in the spirit of Henry
James, to have language do the work of characterization. There is
so much for a novelist to put together before he can invite people
into the world of his imagination; there are so many things to say
about human beings who, in the absence of public beliefs, appear
arbitrary to themselves and to everyone else. The novelist feels he
has to work ten times harder than he used to, falls into despair, and
tries to ram it all home. Things aren't as clear as they used to be,
and there's no kidding ourselves that they are. The true novelist
wants only to set the stage, to get people going, to tell his story, but
as Augie March says, "You do all you can to humanize and famil-
iarize the world, and suddenly it becomes stranger than ever." The
sense of that strangeness is vivid despite the murky powers of contemporary novelists; no wonder, having to make language work all
the time for them, that they often escape into an assumed violence
and negligence of tone.

Sometimes the language of violence fits. Ralph Ellison's *Invisible Man* is a series of episodes, but the screaming crescendo on which
the book opens—the hero in his Harlem cellar, all the stolen lights
ablaze, collaring the reader and forcing him to notice and to hear—
is an unforgettably powerful expression, at the extreme of racial
experience, of the absurdity, the feeling of millions that the world
is always just out of their reach. I don't care for novelists who ignore
what H. G. Wells himself called the "queerness" that has come into
contemporary life since the bomb.

The ways of escape from this queerness are legion, but let me
name some who don't try to escape it. Paul Bowles doesn't, although

his values are so skittery that he sometimes seems to escape from horror into a Fitzpatrick travelogue. The American writer is so likely to see more of the world, and to experience it more openly, that, like Hemingway at the end of *Death in the Afternoon,* he always wants to get in after the bell all the sensuous travel notes he hadn't been able to fit into his book. Bowles tends to fall into this sophisticated romanticism; sometimes he reports North Africa and Asia instead of setting his imagination in them. On the other hand, the landscape in *The Sheltering Sky* itself represents the inhumanity of people who can no longer communicate with one another, the coldness of a world that now seems to put man off. What minimizes the symbolic values in *The Sheltering Sky* and deprives us of the "resonance" we used to get in fiction is the aloneness of people who are concerned entirely with the search for their own sexual satisfaction. The slightly depressing atmosphere of anxiety that hangs over Bowles's novel is characteristic of the effort to find an identity for oneself in sexual relationships. Norman Mailer, a writer with so much more native power than Bowles, with so much more ability to confront American life directly than he seems to acknowledge, has created in *The Deer Park* the same essential atmosphere of paralysis, of the numbness that results when people feel themselves to be lost in the pursuit of compulsions.

Mailer's novels, at least for me, personify the dilemma of novelists who are deeply concerned with history but dangerously oversimplify it; if they seem consumed by their interest in sex it is because they are always seeking some solution for "the times." In many ways Mailer seems to me the most forceful and oddly objective novelist of his age, objective in the sense that he is most capable of imagining objects to which a reader can give himself. You see this, despite the obvious debts to older writers, in *The Naked and the Dead* and in the satire behind the wonderful exchanges between the producer and his son-in-law in *The Deer Park.* Yet Mailer's interest in the external world has dwindled to the point where the theme of sexual power and delight—which Mailer feels to be a lost secret in contemporary life—has become a labyrinthine world in itself.

Mailer now seems bent on becoming the American Marquis de Sade, where once he seemed to be another Dos Passos. Yet the energy, the often unconscious yet meticulous wit, above all the eery and totally unexpected power of concrete visualization are curious because Mailer is able to make more of a world out of his obsessions than other writers are able to make out of the given materials of our common social world.

Here I come to the heart of my complaint. I complain of the dimness, the shadowiness, the flatness, the paltriness, in so many reputable novelists. I confess that I have never been able to get very much from Wright Morris, though he is admired by influential judges. In reading Morris's *The Field of Vision,* I thought of George Santayana's complaint that contemporary poets often give the reader the mere suggestion of a poem and expect him to finish the poem for them. Morris's many symbols, his showy intentions, his pointed and hinted significances, seem to me a distinct example of the literary novel which professors like to teach and would like to write: solemnly meaningful in every intention, but without the breath or extension of life.

There are many writers, like J. D. Salinger, who lack strength, but who are competent and interesting. He identifies himself too fussily with the spiritual aches and pains of his characters; in some of his recent stories, notably "Zooey" and "Seymour: An Introduction," he has overextended his line, thinned it out, in an effort to get the fullest possible significance out of his material. Salinger's work is a perfect example of the lean reserves of the American writer who is reduced to "personality," even to the "mystery of personality," instead of the drama of our social existence. It is the waveriness, the effort at control, that trouble me in Salinger; the professional hand is there, the ability to create an imaginative world, plus almost too much awareness of what he can and can't do. Only, it *is* thin, and peculiarly heartbreaking at times; Salinger identifies the effort he puts out with the vaguely spiritual "quest" on which his characters are engaged, which reminds me of Kierkegaard's saying that we have become "pitiful," like the lace-makers whose work is so flimsy.

The delicate balances in Salinger's work, the anxious striving, inevitably result in beautiful work that is rather too obviously touching, and put together on a frame presented to it by the *New Yorker*.

But I must admit that the great majority of stories I read in magazines seem only stitchings and joinings and colorings of some original model. No wonder that in so much contemporary fiction we are excited by the intention and tolerate the achievement. We are so hungry for something new in fiction that the intention, marked early in the handling of a story, will often please us as if it were the dramatic emotion accomplished by the story; the intuition of hidden significance that usually waits for us at the end of a Salinger story is both a reward to the reader and the self-cherished significance of the story to the writer himself.

Salinger's characters are incomparably larger and more human than those of John Cheever, but Cheever has a gift for being more detached and at the same time more open to what *is*—to the ever-present danger and the half-felt queerness of contemporary existence. It is a pity in a way—I am thinking here of Cheever's stories, not his novel—that contemporary American fiction must derive so much of its strength from the perishable value of social information. James Jones wrote a really extraordinary documentary novel in *From Here to Eternity,* and ever since, like so many Americans who wrote extraordinary first novels directly out of experience, he has had the look of someone trying to invent things that once were conferred on him. So Cheever, in the *New Yorker* style, sometimes takes such easy refuge in the details of gardens, babysitters, parks, dinners, apartment houses, clothes, that he goes to the opposite extreme of the Beat writers (who present the sheer emptiness of life when human beings are not attached to a particular environment): he falls into mechanical habits of documentation, becomes a slyer John O'Hara. It is as if he were trying to get back to the social reportage and satire that worked in our fiction so long as the people writing these stories, like Sinclair Lewis or Scott Fitzgerald, knew what values they could oppose to the "rich." As one can see from O'Hara's novels, which get more pointless as they get bigger and sexier, it is impossible to remain an old-fashioned "realist" unless you can portray a class or an individual opposed to the dominant majority. (James Gould Cozzens was able to do exactly this in *Guard of Honor* but not in *By Love Possessed,* which is more of an aggrieved complaint against the destruction of values.) O'Hara's *Appointment in Samarra* was an exciting book because it involved the real conflict of classes in America; *From the Terrace* suggests that the transformation of our society has proceeded beyond the power of a commonplace mind to describe it deeply. For depth of description demands that the writer identify himself with a social force to which he can give symbolic significance, that he can discern a pattern in history, that he can not only plot his way through it but recognize himself to be a figure in it.

This social intelligence is now lacking to our novelists, except to those brilliant Southern writers, like William Styron and Flannery O'Connor, who can find the present meaningful because they find the past so. But other Southern writers run the risk of being as confused as anyone else once they get off that safe subject, the betrayal of the past, which has been Faulkner's great theme. The bigger, richer, and more anxious the country becomes, the more writers in the traditional mode, like O'Hara, or writers who are now formidably "hip," like Mailer, find themselves trying to find in sex as individual appetite the drama of society in which they can see themselves as partisans and judges. This lack of breadth and extent and dimension I have been complaining of: what is it but the uncertainty of these writers about their connection with that part of reality which other novelists include in their work simply because they are always aware of it—not because they have strained to know it? What many writers feel today is that reality is not much more than what *they* say it is. This is a happy discovery only for genius. For most writers today, the moral order is created, step by step, only through the clarifications achieved by art and, step by step, they refuse to trust beyond the compass of the created work. There has probably never been a time when the social nature of the novel was so much at odds with the felt lack of order in the world about us. In the absence of what used to be *given,* the novelist must create a wholly imaginary world—or else he must have the courage, in an age when personal willfulness rules in every sphere, to say that we are *not* alone, that the individual does not have to invent human values but only to rediscover them. The novel as a form will always demand a common-sense respect for life and interest in society.

Whatever my complaints, I never despair of the novel. As someone said, it is more than a form, it is a literature. I hope never to overlook the positive heroism of those writers who believe in the novel and in the open representation of experience that is its passion and delight—who refuse to believe that there can be an alternative to it for an age like ours. And it does seem to me that the tangibility, the felt reverberations of life that one finds in a writer like Bernard Malamud, spring from his belief that any imaginative "world," no matter how local or strange, *is* the world, and that for the imaginative writer values must be considered truths, not subjective fancies. It is really a kind of faith that accounts for Malamud's "perfect sympathy" with *his* characters in *The Assistant* and *The Magic Barrel.* Though it is difficult for the alone to sympathize with each other, it is a fact that fiction can elicit and prove the world we share, that it can display the unforeseen possibilities of the human—even when everything seems dead set against it.

CHAPTER 3

Poetry's Silver Age

An Improbable Dialogue

STANLEY KUNITZ

[Imagine a college campus in the northeastern United States. The Poet, a nervous chain-smoker, who is concluding a ten-day visit as the guest of the English faculty, is sprawled, with his green bag of books half-emptied on the grass, under a twisted gingko tree. He is somewhat frayed, like his corduroy jacket. His manner is amiable but detached; an ironic formality is his mode of defense. The Young Man who approaches him seems relatively surer of himself, despite his near-sightedness and deferential manner. A slight pink fuzz, of little hirsute promise, adorns his chin.]

YOUNG MAN Pardon me, sir, but did you get a chance to read the manuscripts I left with you yesterday? I'm anxious to hear what you think. It's a lot to ask of you, I know. I hope it wasn't too much of a chore.

POET Not at all! I preferred the shorter poems. Here they are in my bag. I must apologize for spilling some coffee over your verse play, which I didn't have time to finish. It was careless of me.

YOUNG MAN That's all right, sir. I've decided to ditch the play anyhow. It's the sequence of lyrics on Vedanta themes that I particularly wanted you to read. Do you think I have talent?

POET (UNENTHUSIASTICALLY) Yes.

YOUNG MAN So you really think I'll be a poet!

POET It doesn't follow as the night the day. Talent is cheap, you know. One of the attractive features of mediocrity is that you can count on it: mediocrity infallibly begets the mediocre. But you can never be sure what the gifted will do. So many of them go straight to hell. Talent without character is more of a curse than no talent at all.

YOUNG MAN I'm rather surprised—may I say?—to have you raise the moral issue. What about Baudelaire? . . . and Poe? . . . and Byron? . . . and . . . and Genêt?

POET I should have said moral stamina. The morality of art is to endure. It's the capacity to endure that I'm talking of.

YOUNG MAN How *do* poets manage to live nowadays?

POET Poets don't live: they get by.

YOUNG MAN But certainly established poets must earn—

POET They earn surprisingly little. I don't believe there are a dozen serious poets in this country, no matter how famous, who regularly earn as much as five hundred dollars a year from the sale of their poems. To bring in that much, a poet would have to dispose of—I mean sell, not give away to the little magazines—a thousand lines of his precious stuff at fifty cents a line, the standard rate of payment . . . and that's a lot of language!

YOUNG MAN But a poet can do quite well with a book of poems, can't he?

POET "Quite well," even for a poet of acknowledged reputation— I don't mean Eliot or Auden—would be to sell out a hard-cover edition of a thousand copies before it is rushed to the remainder counters. Over the past decade it is unlikely that 5 per cent of the books of contemporary verse issued by regular trade publishers have sold more than six hundred copies apiece. A few poets, the ones who invariably get into textbooks and anthologies, collect some modest additional fees for the permissions. It should be remarked as one of the curiosities of literary life in America that while poets pine, anthologists prosper.

YOUNG MAN I always thought that anthologies did poets a great service. We use one in our contemporary lit class, and it's introduced me to dozens of poets I never even heard about.

POET And perhaps never will again. Anthologies are like wives that can't be lived with or without. Too often they seem to be compiled by men with an ear to the ground, which puts them in a bad position for doing their required homework. Moreover, they tend to perpetuate the kind of poem that is made up of the fashionable floating materials of a period. Most poets are known to the general reading public not by their best or most recent or most characteristic productions but by the pieces, usually inoffensive early ones, that the anthologists redundantly offer. Some of our most distinguished poets have remained relatively obscure for years, even for decades, either through anthological caprice or simply because their work did not seem to lend itself to captivity in the standard zoos of the period.

YOUNG MAN Are you referring to anybody in particular?

POET Phelps Putnam and John Peale Bishop are examples of poets who were under-rated while they were alive. Putnam, in fact, is still relatively unknown. When H. D., who is responsible for creating the image of Imagism, was publicly honored this year, most persons were astonished to learn that she was still extant. Laura Riding, the unconcessive sibyl from whom both Robert Graves and W. H. Auden took lessons in their secret craft, has disappeared into the out-of-print silences. We have a furious prophet in our midst named Edward Dahlberg, who gets the shabby treatment that prophets should expect. Open any popular anthology on your shelf and try to find what tribute is paid to Charles Olson or Kenneth Rexroth, who are potentates in their own right. Because of Robert Penn Warren the novelist, RPW the poet is dismissed into the shade. Yvor Winters, that vehemently entrenched formalist, has yet to enjoy his turn in the limelight—but wait till next year! Theodore Roethke, who in one of his disguises plays demon botanist, our Darwin in the greenhouse of the Id, is a latecomer to the anthologies, still inadequately represented. And then there is Jean Garrigue with her baroque ectasy:

This day is not like that day.
That was a day majestic with clouds,
Barrows of fruit, ices and birds,
And in the pink stalls the melon,
While the mango, magniloquent stem,
Steeped him in baskets, Othello's green,

And there were strawberries, the plums
   and the figs.
This day is not.

These poets I have mentioned—and how can I exclude J. V.
Cunningham and John Berryman and Howard Nemerov from
any list of the undervalued?—have a record of mature achievement. I am not talking of the fledglings.

YOUNG MAN Speaking of fledglings, I wish you would give me a
bit of advice. I'm planning to earn my living by teaching. That
means I'll have to continue with my studies in order to acquire
a Ph.D. Do you approve of a teaching career for poets?

POET Your phrasing disturbs me. If you are a poet, poetry must
be your career. It doesn't matter much what you do to hold your
skin and bones together, so long as you stay intact within. I like
to teach, but try to keep myself mobile, unattached to any specific community of scholars, disaffiliated in the current phrase.
Above all what's essential is to keep the image of yourself as
poet alive. The living poets one can admire have done precisely
that: preserved the image in their mind and mirrored it in their
art. All the other business of the life, no matter how faithfully
transacted, has been subordinated to that image. And by that
image we know them.

YOUNG MAN Robert Frost, William Carlos Williams, T. S. Eliot. . . .

POET Our Senators! Each over seventy—Frost is eighty-four—
and fresher this very day than the downiest workshop graduate
out of Iowa State. On the surface, Frost is the most orthodox
member of the triumvirate, the one who seems to derive most
directly from the familiar poetic tradition in English, which is
essentially bucolic. The Industrial Revolution succeeded in
changing the landscape (mostly by fouling it) overnight; but a
hundred and fifty years, more or less, had to pass before it could
produce a race of unqualifiedly urban poets. As a people we are
still suspicious of this new breed of city poet, whom we profess
not to understand. The truth is that we find them too disturbing to want to understand them: they are associated in our minds
with all the impurities, anxieties, and excesses of metropolitan
existence. Though Frost was not born in the New England coun-
tryside, he had the luck or the genius to become identified with

it. His most successful work of the imagination is the legend he has created about himself. Because of it we tend to picture him at some rural crossroads as proprietor of the general store, dispensing his honest wares with a benevolent seasoning of colloquial salt.

YOUNG MAN You seem to be implying that this homespun quality of his isn't quite genuine.

POET Don't misunderstand me. It is no less genuine in him than it was in old Ben Franklin. It could be argued that the American genius has historically had two natures and two poles—the one idealistic, metaphysical, living in abstraction and pure reason; the other shrewd, practical, individualistic, even self-centered. Emerson and Franklin respectively embody these contradictions. Now Frost, who wins your confidence by insisting that he talks nothing but common sense, is the heir of Franklin, from whom he borrows Poor Richard's voice; but remember that Franklin himself was thoroughly a man of the world. As I remarked before, Frost is not an urban poet, but no one could be further removed from naïveté. His mind is tough and undeceived. Its rather special brand of urbanity is what his art conceals:

Some have relied on what they knew;
Others on being simply true.
What worked for them might work for you.

No memory of having starred
Atones for later disregard,
Or keeps the end from being hard.

Better to go down dignified
With boughten friendship at your side
Than none at all. Provide, provide!

YOUNG MAN Nearly everybody praises Frost, but I don't detect many signs of his influence.

POET He is a presence, a landmark, a touchstone, rather than a direct influence. In any case, who could tolerate a flock of homespun young poets? The young have found it easier to raid Eliot and Williams. For a long time, for more than three decades,

in fact, you could scarcely pick up a poem by a young writer
without overhearing somewhere in the background, however
faintly echoed, the breathless, reiterative, suspended rhythm of
Eliot:

> If the lost word is lost, if the spent word is spent
> If the unheard, unspoken
> Word is unspoken, unheard;
> Still is the unspoken word, the Word unheard,
> The Word without a word, the Word within
> The world and for the world;
> And the light shone in darkness and
> Against the Word the unstilled world still whirled
> About the centre of the silent Word.

Paul-Elmer More said of Emerson that he was "a kind of lay
preacher to the world," and such is Eliot today, the last of the
literary Brahmins, with the same kind of coldly nervous, eclectic,
intellectual force as his predecessor, and with the same gift for
writing memorable quotations. It was Eliot, with the help of
his incorrigible brother-in-art Pound, who made a fashion in
poetry out of irony, wit, indirection, allusiveness, and objec-
tivity. You can see how the fashion persists by examining *New
Poets of England and America,* the quasi-official anthology of the
poets under forty who belong, as of this date, to the literary
establishment.

YOUNG MAN The Beat poets, I've noticed, didn't make the grade for
that collection. That's the penalty they pay, I suppose, for buck-
ing the conventional trend. After Ginsberg and Corso it seems
sort of silly to go back to writing villanelles, don't you think?

POET Hold on there! I haven't finished with the seniors yet. The
last of the triumvirate is William Carlos Williams, Bill Williams
to countless friends and disciples. Others we think of primarily
in terms of their art, but Williams, who has only recently retired
from his general medical practice in New Jersey, assails us first
as a human being, expansive, compassionate, and emancipated.
This is the man whom Wallace Stevens once introduced as having "spent his life in rejecting the accepted sense of things." In his
American lineage he goes back directly to Walt Whitman, but I

don't think it's fanciful to recognize his kinship with the village atheist and Huck Finn and—earlier still—with Natty Bumppo, the staunchly resourceful hero of Cooper's tales of the frontier.

YOUNG MAN The other day in class our professor described Williams as a sort of anti-poet, but I couldn't tell whether he meant it as praise or blame.

POET An ambiguous term certainly, but it has a degree of validity. In at least a score of manifestoes Williams has announced his program of rejecting the clichés of "poetic" feeling and the pomp of a literary language, together with his pet aversion, the iambic foot. Poetry begins for him any day, on the local spot, in the common rhythms of American speech:

Every day that I go out to my car
I walk through a garden
and wished often that Aristotle
had gone on
to a consideration of the dithyrambic
poem—or that his notes had survived
Coarse grass mars the fine lawn

as I look about right and left
tic toc—
And right and left the leaves
upon the yearling peach grow along
the slender stem.

No rose is sure. Each is one rose
and this, unlike another,
opens flat, almost as a saucer without
a cup. But it is a rose, rose
pink. One can feel it turning slowly
upon its thorny stem

YOUNG MAN That rose bothers me. I don't see how it fits into an anti-poet's scheme of values.

POET Why? This is a real, honest-to-God rose, not one of those fake roses that the Romantic poets flung riotously about them when they weren't languishing among the pale lilies.

YOUNG MAN You were saying about the Beat poets that—

POET Was I? My recollection is that I was summing up my impressions of Frost, Eliot, and Williams, whom you can't pluck out of the landscape without wrecking its contours. Incredibly, these are the figures—all born before 1880—who still dominate the scene—along with Stevens, whose reputation remains at zenith after his death; and Pound, the most sparkling of fountainheads (before the madness sullied him); and Marianne Moore, who made imaginary toads with real gardens in them; and—a bit later—E. E. Cummings, juggler and jongleur, the irrepressible one, whom the young have the habit of discovering every spring. What a generation of poets that was! Each name suggests so many others. I think, among the survivors, of Robinson Jeffers, who gave his heart to the hawks—a gesture temporarily out of favor; and of John Crowe Ransom and Allen Tate, who somehow made of poetry a chivalric enterprise; and of Conrad Aiken and Archibald MacLeish, with their gift of indomitable eloquence.

How can one explain that no American poet since the turn of the century has been able thus far to create an equally recognizable public image of himself? The longest shadows are still cast by those poets whose fame dates from the twenties. Perhaps they were so strong and idiosyncratic that their immediate successors, like the children of domineering parents, found it difficult to assert themselves freely. Consider that the most influential new poet of the thirties was Auden; of the forties, Dylan Thomas. It was easier then for a British poet to sound original.

YOUNG MAN I wish I had a better idea of what's going on in England right now. The only newer poets I've read are Peter Larkin and John Betjeman, and they're not so new. I wonder why I keep remembering some lines of Larkin's that go:

No, I have never found
The place where I could say
This is my proper ground,
Here I shall stay;
Nor met that special one
Who has an instant claim
On everything I own
Down to my name. . . .

POET A memorable diffidence! But I think most British verse today seems manufactured for domestic consumption. Auden and Thomas shipped better. Compare those Larkin lines with a stanza from a love poem by Theodore Roethke:

I kiss her moving mouth,
Her swart hilarious skin;
She frolicks like a beast;
And I dance round and round,
A fond and foolish man,
And see and suffer myself
In another being, at last.

The American, you can see, risks more. He even risks making himself ridiculous. As for myself, being an American, I suppose I am committed to the violence within, as Stevens described it, that rises to oppose the violence without. I prefer a poetry that dares to fail.

YOUNG MAN Would you suggest any other young poets for me to read?

POET Any poet in his prime is a young one. Roethke, who is in his early fifties, has been heard to refer to himself as "the oldest younger poet" in America. He is some ten years older than Robert Lowell. After the elders, these are the voices that at this moment make themselves most singularly heard—I am not implying that they are the only ones to have written poems good enough to stand. Of the poets in their thirties, Richard Wilbur, with his hard grace is the first to establish an identity; but I can think of at least a dozen gifted others—W. S. Merwin and Louis Simpson and David Wagoner, and James Wright and W. D. Snodgrass, to begin with—who are impatiently waiting in the wings.

YOUNG MAN I don't know what to think of Lowell's new book, *Life Studies*. Some of it seems to be in pretty bad taste . . . all that embarrassing family stuff. Do you like the poem called "Man and Wife"? It starts with a shocker:

Tamed by Miltown, we lie on Mother's bed . . .

POET I don't have to like it: I'm moved by it. I have the sense, furthermore, of witnessing a preliminary breakthrough into the poetry of the next decade. It's conceivable that Lowell is here recapturing a good portion of the territory that poetry has for so long yielded to the novel:

All night I've held your hand,
as if you had
a fourth time faced the kingdom of the mad—
its hackneyed speech, its homicidal eye—
and dragged me home alive. . . . Oh my *Petite*,
clearest of all God's creatures, still
    all air and nerves:
you were in your twenties, and I
once hand on glass
and heart in mouth,
outdrank the Rahvs in the heat
of Greenwich Village, fainting at your feet—
too boiled and shy
and poker-faced to make a pass,
while the shrill verve
of your invective scorched the traditional South.

Now twelve years later, you turn your back.
Sleepless, you hold
your pillow to your hollows like a child;
your old-fashioned tirade—
loving, rapid, merciless—
breaks like the Atlantic Ocean on my head.

YOUNG MAN I don't wish to sound impertinent, but you keep skirting round the Beat school—I wonder why. After all, they've made the biggest noise of any poets in our time. And their poems, it seems to me, are just as interesting in a confessional way as Lowell's.

POET Noise isn't virtue. It isn't even reputation. How can one talk seriously about a "school" of poets? Poets don't run in packs. And confessions aren't to be confused with public rants and exhibitions. If we are going to bait academic poets—one of the most wholesome of literary sports—we might as well keep in mind that the Beat poets constitute the most clearly denned and most widely publicized "academy" in the American world of poetry today. Allen Ginsberg's *Howl* was an event of a kind, a rhetorical blockbuster, but the subsequent squeals and bleats have become something of a nuisance, as well as a bore.

YOUNG MAN Most of the young intellectuals in college have a touch of the Beat in them. I wouldn't disclaim it myself, as you may have noticed in my poems. My best friend is a practicing Zen Buddhist. We find something there—I don't quite know what it is—that we're looking for.

POET Of course you do. Life, Liberty, and the Pursuit of Nothingness! Demolish the false gods of the West! Worship at the shrine of the jazz Buddha! "The age," wrote Pound in another context, "demanded an image/Of its accelerated grimace." We are getting it: in half-baked nihilism and disheveled mysticism.

The "age demanded" chiefly a mould in plaster,
Made with no loss of time,
A prose kinema, not, not assuredly, alabaster
Or the "sculpture" of rhyme.

YOUNG MAN I had expected you to be more favorably disposed to experimental writing.

POET I am. A writer is either experimental or dead. Most of the writers, however, who insist on labeling themselves in capital letters as experimental are merely betraying their insecurity. Each literary generation requires the existence of an *avant-garde,* not because the latter are more advanced than the writers of reputation, or superior to them, but because the prevailing style of a period needs always to be resisted if it is to maintain its tension, needs always to be modified to keep it supple. Sometimes the nature of the resistance is in effect a backward look, but to a different set of ancestors from those venerated by the mandarins. This happens not to be a time of great innovation in poetic technique: it is rather a period in which the technical gains of past decades, particularly the twenties, are being tested and consolidated. At the moment, for the poets of the Resistance, Williams is the godfather and Pound the Grand Anarch.

YOUNG MAN That's certainly true for the Beat poets.

POET It's equally true for their more obscure cousins, The Black
  Mountain Boys.

YOUNG MAN I'm less familiar with their stuff. That's the group—
  correct me if I'm wrong—led by Charles Olson?

POET Dominated by Olson, yes; just as he in turn is dominated
  by Pound *cum* Lawrence. Robert Creeley, Paul Blackburn, and
  Robert Duncan belong there too, all of them associated at first
  with the *Black Mountain Review* and, more recently, with Jonathan Williams' Jargon Books. Denise Levertov is tenuously
  affiliated. You would have known more about them if they had
  created a scandal. They have a certain pride of craft and of
  separateness.

YOUNG MAN I have a feeling—what with all these little mags
  springing up—that there must be several new interesting clus-
  ters of poets emerging.

POET By the dozen! One I've had some pleasure singling out, though
  it lacks a house organ and has only the loosest kind of cohesive-
  ness, is The New York Gallery Group, consisting of poets associated in one way or another with the abstract expressionist painters
  of the city—the dynamic center of the art world today. These
  poets—Frank O'Hara, Kenneth Koch, and John Ashbery among
  them—write poems on occasion that are full of somersaults
  and Chinese firecrackers. Everything seems absurd—except
  that the game is being played in earnest.

YOUNG MAN So much of the literature of the *avant-garde* seems
  permeated with the concept of the absurd. I've been reading the
  Existentialists, and—

POET Indeed! Metaphysically, the *avant-garde* embraces absurdity; politically, it preaches nihilism; experientially, it prizes the
  instant of sensation; technically, it seeks the fluidity, the open-
  ness, the immediacy of improvisation.

YOUNG MAN What I like about the new work is its spontaneity. I
  never really enjoyed writing until I took to inventing street poems,
  letting myself go, putting down whatever words happen. Some
  of my street poems are my very best work, wouldn't you say?

POET I wouldn't deny that writing tends to freeze into conventional molds. Even a theory of improvisation can develop into a
  convention too. What is desirable is the *effect* of spontaneity—but

the great works aren't likely to fall from the imagination like rain. The process of art always involves a person. On this point Yeats made a memorable comment in an unfamiliar quatrain:

The friends that have it I do wrong
When ever I remake a song,
Should know what issue is at stake:
It is myself that I remake.

YOUNG MAN You remarked a few minutes ago that you like a poetry that takes risks.

POET Yes, exactly. Self-indulgence, automatism, is an escape from the risk of art. The poem does not lie easy in the mind for the picking. It must be fought for intimately through long days and nights, mostly nights. The actual process of composition is a solitary journey to the other side of fatigue and consciousness. There would be no poems if poets did not have boldness, compulsions, cunning, science, and luck.

YOUNG MAN Science seems a strange word for a poet to use in that context.

POET Why? The mind of the scientist, exploring space and matter, is closely related to the mind of the poet, whose task is to explore inner space and the reality of things. Like the scientist the poet is enchanted with an expanding universe of knowledge; but he keeps insisting that the new data must be incorporated into a moral universe, the universe that poetry originally created as myth and is perpetually in the process of re-creating. "After such knowledge, what forgiveness?" asked Eliot. Poets who blindly fight science are ignoring their commitment to the human ultimate. Ideally the mind of the poet is pulled in two ways: on one side, to the purity of the precision of mathematics; on the other, to the purity of the violence of love.

YOUNG MAN Isn't it ironic, in the light of what you're saying, that the poet wins so little recognition today?

POET No more ironic or absurd than most things that happen. Actually, the poet has some reason to be grateful that his work is practically worthless as a commodity. He is unassailed by conflicting standards of value. Unlike the novelist or the dramatist, he is privileged to be exempt from the pressure to modify the quality of his work in order to produce a piece of entertainment. Nothing he can do will make his work profitable. He might as well yield to the beautiful temptation to strive towards an absolute art.

YOUNG MAN But why then does everybody complain about the state of poetry today? Except for poets themselves and would-be poets, who reads poetry anyhow?

POET Despite what I've said before, the audience is larger than you think, much larger than the cash register indicates. I've already mentioned the anthologies that are devoured annually in the tens of thousands by our schools and colleges. The new paperback editions of contemporary poets, particularly those issued by The City Lights Pocket Bookshop of San Francisco and by Grove Press of New York, have already blasted all the traditional publishers' preconceptions about the limitations of the market. Any librarian will tell you that books and periodicals of verse are in constant circulation. *Poetry* of Chicago, I hear, has doubled its subscription list in recent years. Furthermore, a published poet is sure to find friends of his work in almost any city in the country, and these readers of poetry are extraordinarily sympathetic and generous.

The ordeal of the artist, of which we hear so much, is real enough, God knows, but so are his joys. The poets of my acquaintance are doing precisely what they want to do and what they believe they do best. Nobody had to twist their arms to make poets out of them. And there's something else to be said. Despite all the lamentations about the state of poetry in America today, the general level of quality, I dare say, is higher than it ever has been in our literary history. It isn't a Golden Age for several obvious reasons, including the absence of one or two monumental geniuses in their prime to consolidate the poetic energies of the age; but it may very well be a Silver Age. I don't envy the lot of the anthologist of the future when he tries to cut the lyrics representing this century down to what he considers a reasonable number. My guess is—my wild guess, if you will—that only the Elizabethan Age will make a better showing.

YOUNG MAN You don't say! I'm impressed by the small battalion of poets you've already named, and it just occurs to me that you haven't even mentioned, among the elders, somebody as famous as Carl Sandburg.

POET Perhaps because he seems to rest so comfortably in his period.

YOUNG MAN Or, among the poets in their middle years, Karl Shapiro and Delmore Schwartz, on whom I wrote a comparative paper recently under the title of "Plato's Cave."

POET My error! Nor have I mentioned three fine women poets—forgive that stupid category!—Louise Bogan, Leonie Adams, and Elizabeth Bishop. Nor Kenneth Fearing and Richard Eberhart and Randall Jarrell, who have nothing in common save that some of their work will not readily be forgotten. Nor the poets who are also masterful translators—what a blaze of activity there!—such as Robert Fitzgerald and Dudley Fitts and Richmond Lattimore and William Arrowsmith and Horace Gregory and Rexroth (whom I *did* mention) and Rolfe Humphries and John Ciardi. As for the very latest crop of writers, I'll have to leave them to you and to their own destinies.

YOUNG MAN I'll admit it's hard to distinguish them yet. . . . One last question, sir. How do publishers feel about accepting a book of verse by a new poet?

POET Frankly, they feel sick at the thought. But it should be noted that two or three years ago they felt worse. Some of the most successful trade publishers have not even considered it scandalous to admit they were disinclined to read *any* manuscripts of verse submitted to them; but recently there have been signs, on the part of several firms, of a re-examination of this policy of abdication. At the moment it would seem that the qualified young writer has his best chance for publication in years, what with the emergence of several bright and adventurous new firms, the growing interest of the university presses in poetry, the proliferation of paperback issues and chap-books, and the availability of new grants and subsidies for this very purpose. Certainly the poet is making himself heard, literally heard, through readings and recordings as never before in modern times. Perhaps the spoken word is about to break down the barrier between the poet and his potential audience. And perhaps even the publishing fraternity is beginning to realize that poetry is the source, the seminal impulse, of all literature, the circumfluent air that gives all the arts of an epoch their weather. Without poetry there would be no literature, no civilization . . . and (to end with a dying fall) no publishers. I have no patience with the Midas-fingered who complain that poetry resists being turned into gold. It is better than gold.

YOUNG MAN Thank you so much, sir, for all the nice things you've said about my manuscript, May I have it back, please?

POET With pleasure.

CHAPTER 4

Why American Plays Are Not Literature

Robert Brustein

One of the unique features of postwar American drama is its cheerful isolation from a central literary tradition. A successful playwright today may think, of himself as a craftsman, an entertainer, even a creative artist, but only in very rare cases would he call himself a literary man. He does not share at all in those common interests—few enough in our society—which unite the novelist, poet, and essayist. In his subject matter, his writing style, his associations, his attitudes, and his ideas, the dramatist is far removed, if not completely cut off, from the mainstream of intellectual and literary discourse.

This lack of communication with the other disciplines gives the drama a peculiar insularity. The typical American playwright is encouraged to write, not by the pull of literary ideals, but by the stimulus of successful Broadway plays, and it is unusual when he develops beyond a hackneyed imitation of what is current and fashionable. Making his friends mainly within the theatrical profession, he rarely ventures out of it to have his mind refreshed. Unlike the novelist, he is almost never represented in the literary periodicals, and when he does communicate with the outside world it is generally through a short piece in the *New York Times* advertising his coming play with a reminiscence about how it came to be written.

Even our most important dramatists, past and present, have tended to remain firmly fixed within the confines of their own experience and craft. Besides plays, all the great European playwrights of the past hundred years wrote poetry, epics, novels, short stories, essays, or criticism; and in modern times dramatists like Brecht, Duerrenmatt, Beckett, Giraudoux, Synge, and O'Casey have moved freely among the other literary disciplines. With the exceptions of Thornton Wilder, Tennessee Williams (both former highbrows), and Arthur Miller, few American playwrights have made more than token gestures in the direction of nondramatic literatures, while even fewer are aware of what is being attempted or said there. Specialization in America, insofar as it has affected the arts, has hit the drama hardest of all, cutting it off not only from other literary traditions but from the very life which should be its subject matter.

This isolation can be partly attributed to the fact that American drama is a comparatively new expression, forced to create its tradition as it goes along. English playwrights like Wilde, Shaw, Eliot, and Osborne could draw on an already established dramatic heritage, one which includes the most distinguished names in literary history; in consequence, even minor dramatists like Barrie, Fry, Bridie, and Galsworthy, nourished by this strain, have created dramatic works which are eminently readable. The American drama, on the other hand—which seems to have sprung full-grown from the imagination of Eugene O'Neill—can still remember its own origins. In fact, O'Neill's persistent experimentation would seem to indicate that he was hurriedly trying to create a dramatic tradition for America which, like their gardens, took the English hundreds of years to produce. Borrowing from the drama of the Greeks, the Elizabethans, the Japanese, and nineteenth-century Europeans, O'Neill sought not native but cosmopolitan influences, and thus initiated a split from American literature which widens every year.

The split, of course, cuts both ways: American literary culture generally scorns the stage. In France, it is a rare thing when a novelist, poet, or philosopher does not express his themes in dramatic form, and it has long been the tradition for a French man of letters to include a volume or two of dramatic essays among his collected writings.

In America, on the other hand, theater criticism, abdicated by most intellectuals, has fallen into the hands of newspaper reviewers, while the drama itself is practically monopolized by commercial playwrights. Although the plays of writers like Camus, Sartre, Gide, Claudel, Mauriac, and Cocteau constitute an important part of their creative work, gifted American authors have, up till now, usually either ignored the drama totally or written badly in it. The quality of Fitzgerald's "The Vegetable," Hemingway's "The Fifth Column," and Wolfe's "Manner-house"—so far inferior to these authors' nondramatic works—would seem to indicate that, unlike their French counterparts, American writers have not regarded the drama as a serious alternative form for the expression of their deepest convictions and insights.

If the American literary man has generally been indifferent, patronizing, or hostile toward the drama, some of the reasons for this indicate why our plays are so often outside the boundaries of literature. For there is a widespread conviction among men of mind that the dramatist, writing for an audience with debased values, does not have very high standards himself—and anxious to please a wide number, he creates a contaminated work which gives literature a bad name. Since the very structure of the drama is dependent on climactic emotional effects, it has often been accused of a fondness for bombast and sensationalism and of lacking intelligence and restraint—"an unmannerly daughter, showing a bad education," wrote Sir Philip Sidney hundreds of years ago, which "causeth her mother Poesy's honesty to be called in question." More frequently content to follow public taste than to lead it, the drama has developed an unsavory reputation through its alliance with the market place.

These traditional objections have become more vigorous in our own time as the drama has sought wider and less discriminating audiences. In the eighteenth century, when a play attracted a public for 62 performances, it was called the most prodigious success in history, while today a play must run for at least a year simply to make up costs. The noncreative unions, the press agents, managers, stagehands, and musicians, are squeezing the theater to death with excessive financial demands, and Broadway further exacerbates the situation with increasingly spectacular and expensive scenic effects guaranteed to excite spectator interest if all else fails. The producer—rather than speculate on something risky and new—sticks to a tried-and-true formula based on the successes of the past. With the drama arbitrated by "show business," questions of finance overrule questions of taste, and it becomes harder to find financial support for anything which might "disturb" the audience.

The dramatist, as a result, discovers a number of non-literary partners looking over his shoulder as he writes, and this makes his work more than ever vulnerable to charges of artistic compromise. Compromise is not an essential of the collaborative enterprise—imagine the conductor of a symphony orchestra dictating elaborate changes in a musical composition for the sake of greater audience appeal. But it has now become second nature to Broadway, and few plays ever open there without having undergone strenuous revisions. While the novelist creates in the solitude of his own imagination, the dramatist re-creates with five or six worried production men at his elbow. Once paramount in importance, the playwright, in consequence, now finds his position overshadowed by the director whose power mushrooms every day; and even some of our most influential dramatists have been known to alter their work radically to retain the interest of a director who might insure its commercial success.

Since these alterations almost invariably result in a work of diminished honesty and complexity, writers whose artistic conscience demands greater satisfactions than commercial reward and the praise of newspaper reviewers view the theater with alarm and suspicion. Archibald MacLeish is one of the few authors, not a professional playwright, who has regarded his occasional stage experience as a happy one, but then he seems to have adjusted nicely to the values of the medium in which he worked:

"I thought I was going to weep [when I heard] the Atkinson review [of 'J.B.']," he writes in a published letter to Kazan, and adds that the critical reception of the play was "general evidence that the problems *were* solved." When a work is primarily evaluated—as it is in our theater—by the enthusiastic applause of the majority, this is evidence indeed, and the distortions and convulsions to which a playwright's original ideas are submitted can be justified by a long line at the box office.

A very different response to theater experience comes from William Gibson, a literary man who looks on the success of his play, "Two for the Seesaw," as a hollow achievement reached by suppressing his true capabilities. Gibson, primarily a poet and novelist, has recorded his agonizing experience in *The Seesaw Log,* an illuminating account of the play's progress from idea to opening night. Like most literary men, "it had been several years since [he] had taken a believing interest in the theater," but once having written a play his ultimate disenchantment was to come when he discovered as his collaborators not only the director, the producer, and the star, but the elevator man and probably the lavatory attendant as well. He found that the perpetual revisions ordered in his play served only to cheapen it; and his original work eventually turned into a harmless diversion giving neither difficulty nor offense to anyone in the theater:

> Fifteen years earlier, when my work consisted of unpublished poems and a magazine asked me to change a word in one, I would not change a word; the poem went unpublished; it was a far cry to the present spate of rewriting to please. . . . I felt this of all of us, that in outgrowing our guardian angelship, and becoming reasonable citizens, we had lost some religious component in ourselves and this component was the difference between art and entertainment. . . . The theater, in this country, in this decade, [is] primarily a place not in which to be serious, but in which to be likeable.

Although one may question why he himself did not resist this cheapening process, Mr. Gibson has accurately defined not only what distinguishes art from entertainment but literature from current drama. The silhouette of show business imposes itself on almost every work for our stage, and Broadway maintains its compulsive need to send the audience home in an affable frame of mind no matter what violence is done to the meaning of the play. With the writer constantly badgered to turn his play into the theatrical equivalent of a best seller, honest works of the imagination invariably become tainted with sentiment and dishonesty.

The director, of course, has a duty to request clarification of an author when his work is muddy, but more frequently revisions are a surrender to commodity demands. The famous changes in the last act of "Cat on a Hot Tin Roof," for example, had no bearing on the essential flaw of the play (which was the elusive ambiguity of the homosexual theme) but they did introduce into a bleak work a hopeful note of uplift compatible with Broadway's desire to remain well liked. The trespassing of the director on the playwright's domain creates an atmosphere in which dramatic literature is very rarely produced, and it remains the knottiest artistic dilemma of the American stage. It is not to be solved, as Tennessee Williams suggests, by having a "good psychiatrist in attendance at rehearsals," but rather by the playwright's strong resistance to commercial pressures when he is certain his work is being cheapened.

Of course, this resistance alone will not guarantee a play of high literary value. American drama is plagued by internal problems as well as external ones, and the dramatist will have to revise a number of his own attitudes if he wishes to create works of lasting power. One of these is his indifference to language. American drama, no matter how serious in intent, is very rarely readable, for our plays are often stage mechanisms which seem oddly wan and listless on the printed page. Only Tennessee Williams has consistently created a dramatic language which a good novelist might not be ashamed to have written, and even his style deteriorated in his last play. Most of our other playwrights, including our greatest, Eugene O'Neill, are charter members of a cult of inarticulacy, communicating high moments of thought and feeling not through speech but through dashes and exclamation points.

Playwrights are generally aware of this problem but do not consider it very important. Ever since the Elizabethan age, dramatists have been embarrassed when their plays appeared in print, but in the past they apologized for literary failings—today they caution the reader to ignore them and concentrate on dramatic values. Elmer Rice, who holds that "literary excellence is not an essential criterion in the evaluation of a play," goes even further in declaring that "words are not even necessary for the creation and communication of drama." Arthur Miller writes: "It is necessary to separate the drama from what we think of today as literature. A drama ought not to be looked at first and foremost from literary perspectives merely because it uses words, verbal rhythms, and poetic image." And Tennessee Williams defiantly defends "the incontinent blaze of a live theater, a theater meant for seeing and feeling." It is not surprising that Eugene O'Neill once blamed the failure of an early play on the fact that the actors had not emphasized the *silences* in the last act where the meaning of the play was to be found.

To emphasize the drama's distinctness from literature is a defensible position if not carried too far. It is certainly true that plays are written primarily to be performed, and that writers who put inordinate emphasis on language to the exclusion of other important dramatic values have invariably produced works which are lifeless and dull on the stage. (I am thinking not only of closet dramatists like Robert Browning, Thomas Hardy, and Henry James but also of working playwrights like Sean O'Casey, whose later plays bog down in a slough of rhetoric.) But both the finely jeweled style of closet drama and the shoddy language of our current plays are extremes. The dramatic form has always seemed to me the greatest literary form because it combines action *and* words. All of the great working dramatists of the past and present have been able to articulate their works, and there is still no better stage device than language for the unfolding of character and the revelation of dramatic insights. By permitting some scenes to be built out of actors' improvisations, certain playwrights abdicate their function entirely; and it is partly because of the playwright's indifference to language that our most conspicuous stage hero is brutal, inarticulate, and incapable of reflecting on his condition. The failure of dramatic language leads to a situation where a great many of our plays, including two of Mr. Miller's, conclude on a question—"Why?"—when it has traditionally been the dramatist's job to answer this question.

In other words, the murky language of our plays is a serious failing only insofar as it reflects our drama's basic failing, its murky thought. American plays are difficult to read because they so often yield little sense when they are read; in the quiet of the study one stumbles on inconsistencies, disharmonies, and contradictions which are sometimes ignored in the rapid excitement of performance. Those dramatists who are aware of this make an oblique admission of it by employing extra-dramatic techniques in the published plays in order to obscure the flaws. In some of the early plays of Eugene O'Neill, for example, extravagant stage directions are provided to sharpen points which have not been suitably dramatized, and Tennessee Williams also is sometimes given to lengthy parenthetical discussions of purpose, especially when he realizes he has ducked the very questions that his play has posed. As George Orwell has proved so emphatically, there is an intimate connection between language and ideas, and inadequate writing is often a sign either of confusion or evasion. In his compulsion to "move" the spectator no matter what happens to credibility or coherence, the American dramatist is further cut off from a literary tradition which is in our time experiencing an authentic renascence distinguished by its involvement with ideas.

As a consequence, American drama often seems to be the most mindless form of legitimate culture since eighteenth-century sentimental comedy, a form to which it bears more than a little resemblance.* I know of few professional American playwrights—Arthur Miller is a prominent exception—who would not consider it very

---

*I quote from Oliver Goldsmith who, in attacking the sentimental dramatists in 1772, might have been describing American domestic plays like "The Dark at the Top of the Stairs" or "Raisin in the Sun": "These comedies have had of late a great success, perhaps from their novelty, and also from their flattering every man in his favorite foible. In these plays almost all die characters are good, and exceedingly generous. . . . If they happen to have faults or foibles, the spectator is taught, not only to pardon, but to applaud them, in consideration of die goodness of their hearts."

odd to be called a thinker. On the contrary, most playwrights are devoted to dramatizing sensations which grow more hysterical and rarefied with every passing year.

In this, no doubt, they are trying to distinguish their work from what they consider the passionlessness of the English theater, and their vitality and energy have often had great value.

But this reaction can be carried too far. Tennessee Williams, for example—who calls himself a "feeling playwright"—is now indifferent to those dramatic works which, in embodying thought, are meant not only for performance but for reading and reflection, for he has developed an entirely different concept of a play:

> The color, the grace and levitation, the structural pattern in motion, and quick interplay of live beings, suspended like fitful lightning in a cloud, these things are the play, not words on paper, nor thoughts and ideas of an author, those shabby things snatched off basement counters at Gimbel's.

Beginning with a distaste for the logical, the abstruse, and the tendentious, Williams concludes by rejecting ideas altogether. He thus turns a truth into a half-truth, for there is a fruitful area between the ideological play and the play of pure sensation. In this area, two of Mr. Williams' major influences, Strindberg and D. H. Lawrence, produced some of their finest work. In fact, Mr. Williams' own place in the drama is secure not only because of his powerful "feeling" but because certain of his plays embodied provocative themes, while much of his later work is inferior because in relying too much on "fitful lightning" his thought became turgid and confused.

It should be clear that to introduce serious thought into the theater is not to rob it of passion; it is rather, by making that passion more meaningful, to impose greater burdens on the audience than a mere fingering of their emotions. I use the qualifying word "serious" because thought of one kind or another exists whether you like it or not—no work which uses words and action can be totally free from ideas. Even the most unintellectual forms, such as the farces of Labiche, have an idea at their base, if only a maxim by La Rochefoucauld. Broadway is depressing not because ideas are not enunciated there but because these ideas invariably *are* "snatched off basement counters at Gimbel's." Pretentious, evasive, and rarely free from formula, the falsification of Broadway thought inevitably results in the falsification of its passion.

Our farces are no longer amoral and destructively funny but now embody homilies and sentiment while our melodramas revolve around drug addiction or the pernicious psychic influence of Mom. Our serious drama is informed by a debased Freudianism, our comedies are set in motion by man-chasing women, and our musicals, with one or two exceptions, are produced by people who write about Love while thinking about Money. There are hardly two plays each year which are not obsessively biological in their themes, yet for all this preoccupation none have any real sexual interest. Homosexuality, promiscuity, infidelity, incest—all these considerations are toyed with but always sentimentalized or evaded. The result is that we have a theater which will not admit the simple truths that everyone discusses in the living-room.

Almost all of our drama, in fact, is equivocal or needlessly ambiguous, for our dramatists find it difficult to square the passionate aspects of their plays with their ideas about American life. One frequently finds, consequently, contradictions between the psychological and the social or the emotional and mental aspects of a play. O'Neill squeezes an attack on American capitalism into a romantic play about Marco Polo; Arthur Miller tries to document the effect of McCarthyism on the American public through an obfuscating treatment of the Salem witch trials; Tennessee Williams drags a Southern segregationist into the middle of a sexual nightmare; and Archibald MacLeish superimposes his feelings about the hydrogen bomb on a religious drama adapted from the Book of Job.

Though each of these dramatists is concerned with some specific fact of American life, none is able to speak concretely about it for fear that his work will somehow lose its "universality"; but as any good literary man can tell them nothing is more "universal" than a careful presentation of the particular. (Saul Bellow's Chicago Jew, Augie March, is more American in his special and concrete experience than any of the universalized figures of our postwar drama.) A direct confrontation of American life—banished from our stage—has had to find refuge in "illegitimate" theatrical entertainments like the monologues of Mort Sahl, the night club skits of May and Nichols, and an occasional review at the Downstairs Room.

There is, in other words, very little that is contemporary about our contemporary drama. Most of our plays, for all the light they throw on American life, might have been written by a Visigoth in the Year 1, while the others merely parrot the liberal prejudices of the audience or hide their meaning (if it is disturbing or controversial) under a mountain of allegory. In this self-imposed censorship, our dramatists demonstrate the most severe consequences of their alienation from intellectual discourse; for in our theater, as it is now constituted, there is little to stimulate the more ambitious playwright. Postwar American drama is stationary, and its fondness for formal experimentation (generally designed to obscure sentiment, banality, or sheer confusion) merely gives it an illusion of movement. America today has no theatrical *avant-garde,* only two dramatists worthy of note, and no one among the younger writers to ruffle a few feathers with radical and exciting new ideas. The intellectual ferment provided in the past by O'Neill, Odets, and Lillian Hellman is practically nonexistent today, and our drama is daily growing more narrow and circumscribed, strangling itself in its own living-room.

Arthur Miller is the one American playwright with the ambition to write a mature drama which transcends the family crisis, the sexual conflict, and the individual psychosis; yet in his utterances about "the people" and "the common man" he sometimes sounds as if his social thinking has not yet progressed past the thirties. Since he is an artist with substantial gifts and a real affection for ideas, it seems a waste that some of his own plays should suffer from the very defects he observes in the plays of others; and it is very possible that these defects might have been avoided or overcome if there had been more opportunity for debate, conversation, and intercourse with his equals in the other disciplines.

I harp on these interdisciplinary influences not just to make an academic point but because there is evidence that American drama may soon be refreshed from nondramatic sources. The younger novelists of the fifties, whose work has such distinction and intelligence, are beginning to show some inclination to knock down the prevailing borders between literature and the drama. Norman Mailer and James Baldwin are both writing plays which are certain, in different ways, to be exciting and unusual; and Lillian Hellman and Lester Osterman are currently encouraging writers like Saul Bellow, Herbert Gold, and James Purdy to write plays as well.

If these writers can transfer to the stage some of the incisive knowledge of American life they display in their novels, if they can submit themselves to the fearfully difficult discipline of the dramatic form,* and if producers can be found who will support their works without trying to commercialize them, we may soon have a substantial group of exciting and controversial playwrights. Even more, we may soon have a drama which will set new standards of honesty, intelligence, and excellence for our practicing playwrights, and which will turn the theater once again into a place not just to be likable but serious and profound.

---

* Saul Bellow's excellent one act play, "The Wrecker," certainly indicates that he already has a native feeling for and understanding of the drama.

CHAPTER 5

The Decline of Book Reviewing

Elizabeth Hardwick

There used to be the notion that Keats was killed by a bad review, that in despair and hopelessness he turned his face to the wall and gave up the struggle against tuberculosis. Later evidence has shown that Keats took his hostile reviews with a considerably more manly calm than we were taught in school, and yet the image of the young, rare talent cut down by venomous reviewers remains firmly fixed in the public mind.

The reviewer and critic are still thought of as persons of dangerous acerbity, fickle demons, cruel to youth and blind to new work, bent upon turning the literate public away from freshness and importance out of jealousy, mean conservatism, or whatever. Poor Keats were he living today might suffer a literary death, but it would not be from attack; instead he might choke on what Emerson called a "mush of concession." In America, now, oblivion, literary failure, obscurity, neglect—all the great moments of artistic tragedy and misunderstanding—still occur, but the natural conditions for the occurrence are in a curious state of camouflage, like those decorating ideas in which wood is painted to look like paper and paper to look like wood. A genius may indeed go to his grave unread, but he will hardly have gone to it unpraised. Sweet, bland commendations fall everywhere upon the scene; a universal, if somewhat lobotomized, accommodation reigns. A book is born into a puddle of treacle; the brine of hostile criticism is only a memory. Everyone is found to have "filled a need," and is to be "thanked" for something and to be excused for "minor faults in an otherwise excellent work." "A thoroughly mature artist" appears many times a week and often daily; many are the bringers of those "messages the Free World will ignore at its peril."

The condition of popular reviewing has become so listless, the effect of its agreeable judgments so enervating to the general reading public that the sly publishers of *Lolita* have tried to stimulate sales by quoting *bad* reviews along with, to be sure, the usual, repetitive good ones. (Orville Prescott: "*Lolita* is undeniably news in the world of books. Unfortunately it is bad news." And Gilbert Highet: "I am sorry that *Lolita* was ever published. I am sorry it was ever written.")

It is not merely the praise of everything in sight—a special problem in itself—that vexes and confounds those who look closely at the literary scene, but there is also the unaccountable sluggishness of the *New York Times* and *Herald Tribune* Sunday book-review sections. The value and importance of individual books are dizzily inflated, in keeping with the American mood at the moment, but the book-review sections as a cultural enterprise are, like a pocket of unemployment, in a state of baneful depression insofar as liveliness and interest are concerned. One had not thought they could go downward, since they have always been modest, rather conventional journals. Still, there had been room for a decline in the last few years and the opportunity has been taken. A Sunday morning with the book reviews is often a dismal experience. It is best to be in a state of distracted tolerance when one takes up, particularly, the *Herald Tribune Book Review*. This publication is not just somewhat mediocre; it has also a strange, perplexing inadequacy as it dimly comes forth week after week.

For the world of books, for readers and writers, the torpor of the *New York Times Book Review* is more affecting. There come to mind all those high-school English teachers, those faithful librarians and booksellers, those trusting suburbanites, those bright young men and women in the provinces, all those who believe in the judgment of the *Times* and who need its direction. The worst result of its decline is that it acts as a sort of hidden dissuader, gently, blandly, respectfully denying whatever vivacious interest there might be in books or in literary matters generally. The flat praise and the faint dissension, the minimal style and the light little article, the absence of involvement, passion, character, eccentricity—the lack, at last, of the literary tone itself—have made the *New York Times* into a provincial literary journal, longer and thicker, but not much different in the end from all those small-town Sunday "Book Pages." (The *New Yorker, Harper's,* the *Atlantic,* the news and opinion weeklies, the literary magazines all devote a good deal of space and thought to the reviewing of books. The often awkward and the always variable results should not go unremarked. However, in these magazines the reviews are only a part of the claim upon the reader's attention, and the peculiar disappointments of the manner in which books are sometimes treated cannot be understood without a close study of each magazine as a whole.)

It is with dismay that one decides the malaise of the popular reviewing publications—the *Times* and *Tribune* and the *Saturday Review*—is not always to be laid at the door of commerce. It had been simple and reassuring to believe the pressure of book publishers and booksellers accounted for the hospitable reception of trashy novels, commonplace "think" books, and so on. The publishers needed favorable reviews to use for the display of their product, as an Easter basket needs shredded green paper under the eggs. No one thought the pressure was simple and direct; it was imagined to be subtle, practical, basic, that is, having to do with the fact that the advertisements of the publishing business keep the book-review sections going financially. This explanation has, naturally, had an exaggerated acceptance.

The truth is, one imagines, that the publishers—seeing their best and their least products received with a uniform equanimity—must be aware that the drama of the book world is being slowly, painlessly killed. Everything is somehow alike, whether it be a routine work of history by a respectable academic, a group of platitudes from the Pentagon, a volume of verse, a work of radical ideas, a work of conservative ideas. Simple "coverage" seems to have won out over the drama of opinion; "readability," a cozy little word, has taken the place of the old-fashioned requirement of a good, clear prose style, which is something else. All differences of excellence, of position, of form are blurred by the slumberous acceptance. The blur erases good and bad alike, the conventional and the odd, so that it finally appears that the author like the reviewer really does not have a position. The reviewer's grace falls upon the rich and the poor alike; a work which is going to be a best seller, in which the publishers have sunk their fortune, is commended only at greater length than the book from which the publishers hardly expect to break even. In this fashion there is a sort of democratic euphoria that may do the light book a service but will hardly meet the needs of a serious work. When a book is rebuked, the rebuke is usually nothing more than a quick little jab with the needle, administered in the midst of therapeutic compliments. "———— ———— is sometimes self-consciously arch," said one review. "But it contains enough of ———— ————'s famous wit and style to make American publication worthwhile. . . ."

The editors of the reviewing publications no longer seem to be engaged in literature. Books pile up, out they go, and in comes the review. Many distinguished minds give their names to various long and short articles in the *Times, Tribune,* and *Saturday Review.* The wares offered by the better writers are apt, frequently, to be something less than their best. Having awakened to so many gloomy Sundays, they accept their assignments in a co-operative spirit and return a "readable" piece, nothing much, of course. (Alice James wrote in her diary that her brother, Henry, was asked to write for the popular press and assured he could do anything he pleased "so long as there's nothing literary in it.")

The retention of certain disgruntled, repetitive commentators is alone enough to dispute notions of crude commercialism on the part of the reviewing publications. A businesslike editor, a "growing" organization—such as we are always reading about in the press— would have assessed the protests, if any, and put these fumbling minds out to pasture. For instance, what could be more tiresome than J. Donald Adams's attacks on poor Lionel Trilling for trying to be interesting on Robert Frost? Only another attack on Adams, perhaps—who is, like the pressure of commerce, hardly the real trouble with the *Times*. Adams is like one of those public monuments only a stranger or someone who has been away for a while takes notice of. "What is truly dismaying about the *Times* and *Tribune* is the quality of the editing.

Recently a small magazine called the *Fifties* published an interview with the editor-in-chief of the *New York Times Book Review*, Mr. Francis Brown. Mr. Brown appears in this exchange as a man with considerable editorial experience in general and very little "feel" for the particular work to which he has been appointed, that is editor of the powerfully important weekly *Book Review*. He, sadly, nowhere in the interview shows a vivid interest or even a sophistication about literary matters, the world of books and writers—the very least necessary for his position. His approach is modest, naïve, and curiously spiritless. In college, he tells us in the interview, he majored in history and subsequently became general editor of *Current History*. Later he went to *Time*, where he had "nothing to do with books," and at last he was chosen to "take a crack at the *Book Review*." The interviewer, hinting at some of the defects of the *Book Review*, wondered if there wasn't too much reliance on specialists, a too frequent practice of giving a book to a reviewer who had written a book like it, or about the same country or the same period. Mr. Brown felt that "a field was a field." When asked to compare our *Times Book Review* with the *Times Literary Supplement* in London, Brown opined, "They have a narrow audience and we have a wide one. I think in fiction they are doing the worst of any reputable publication."

This is an astonishing opinion to anyone who has followed the reviews in the London *Times* and the other English reviewing papers, such as the Sunday *Times* and the *Observer*. These papers consistently set a standard intrinsically so much higher than ours that detailed comparison is almost impossible. It is not simply what may turn up in an individual review; it is profoundly a matter of the tone, the seriousness, the independence of mind and temperament. Richard Blackmur in a recent article tells of a conversation with the editor of the *Times Literary Supplement* who felt that the trouble with the American book reviews was just this lack of a strong, independent editorial direction and who ventured that very few publishers would withdraw their advertising because of the disappearance of the bland product being put out at the moment. A description of the *Times Literary Supplement,* the London publication, by Dwight Macdonald finds that the English paper "seems to be edited and read by people who know who they are and what interests them. That the vast majority of their fellow citizens do not share their interest in the development of English prose, the bibliography of Byelorussia, Andre Gide's treatment of his wife, the precise relation of folksong and plainsong, and 'the large blot' in a letter of Dr. Johnson's which has given much trouble to several of his editors . . . this seems not in any way to trouble them."

Invariably right opinion is not the only judge of a critic's powers, although a taste that goes wrong frequently is only allowed to the greatest minds! In any case, it all depends upon who is right and who is wrong. The communication of the delight and importance of books, ideas, culture itself, is the very least one would expect from a journal devoted to reviewing of new and old works. Beyond that beginning, the interest of the mind of the individual reviewer is everything. Book reviewing is a form of writing. We don't pick up the Sunday *Times* to find out what Mr. Smith thinks of, for instance, *Dr. Zhivago*. (It would very likely be *Mrs.* Smith in the *Herald Tribune*.) As the saying goes, What do you have when you find out what Mr. Smith thinks of *Dr. Zhivago?* It *does* matter what an unusual mind, capable of presenting fresh ideas in a vivid and original and interesting manner, thinks of books as they appear. For sheer information, a somewhat expanded publisher's list would do just as well as a good many of the reviews that appear weekly.

In a study of book reviewing done at Wayne University, we find that our old faithful, the eternally "favorable review," holds his own with all the stamina we have learned to expect. Fifty-one per cent of the reviews summarized in *Book Review Digest* in 1956 were favorable. A much more interesting figure is that 44.3 per cent were *non-committal!* The bare meaning of "review" would strongly incline most people to the production of an opinion of some sort and so the reluctance of the non-committal reviewers to perform is a fact of great perplexity. The unfavorable reviews number 4.7 per cent.

A Sunday some months ago in the *Herald Tribune.* The following are excerpts from five reviews of current novels, reviews that sadly call to mind a teen-age theme.

(1) "The real value of the novel lies in its awareness of character, the essential personality, and the subtle effect of time."

(2) "Occasionally some of the workings of the story seem contrived, but this is only a first impression, for foremost of all is the re-creation of an atmosphere which is so strong that it dictates a destiny."

(3) "Miss ———— writes well, telling the story with a matter-of-factness and vividness that help to carry the strangeness of her central theme. For a reader who relishes a touch of the macabre, it is an intriguing exploration of the imagination."

(4) "———— ————, however, is an interesting and swiftly moving book; more complicated than most of its kind, and with subtler shading to its characters. It makes good reading."

(5) "It is also, within the framework ———— ———— has set for himself, a warm, continuously interesting story of what can happen to a group of ordinary people in a perilous situation, a situation, incidentally, at least as likely as the one Nevil Shute postulates in 'On the Beach.'"

("The one Nevil Shute postulates in 'On the Beach'"—the assurance of this phrase would give many a reader a pause, reminding us, as it does, that there are all kinds of examples of what is called "obscurity of reference.")

About the *Saturday Review,* one feels more and more hat it is not happy in its job. It is moody, like an actress looking for the right role in order to hit the big time. "Of literature" has been dropped from the title, an excision he miscellaneous contents of the magazine soundly justifies. The search for feature ideas is as energetic as that of any national magazine; the editors are frantically trying to keep up with the times. With the huge increase in phonograph-record sales, the music departments have absorbed more and more space in the journal. Travel, in all its manifestations, has become an important concern—travel books, travel advice, guides to nearly as many events as *Cue* tries to handle. Even this is not enough. There are lacing Car issues and SR Goes to the Kitchen. Extraordinary promotion ideas occur to the staff, such as the *Saturday Review Annual Advertising Award.* Lines from an article on this topic read:

Because *Saturday Review* is continually concerned with the communications pattern in the United States, it has observed with deep interest the progressive development of advertising as a medium of idea communication, a much more subtle skill even than the communication of news.

The cover may "feature" a photograph of Joanne Woodward and recently in an issue that featured Max Eastman's written ideas on Hemingway, not Eastman, but Hemingway, wearing a turtle-neck sweater, gazed from the cover in a "photo-portrait." The book reviews, the long and the short articles, in *Saturday Review* are neither better nor worse than those of the *Times;* they are marked by the same lack of strenuous effort. They obviously have their audience in mind—one, it is believed, that will take only so much.

Literary journalism reaches, in the case of a good many writers, such levels of vitality and importance and delight that the excuse of the fleeting moment, the pressure of time, the needs of a large public cannot be accepted, as the editors would have us do. Orville Prescott of the daily *Times*—is he to be accounted a casualty of speed? Is what is wanting in this critic simply time to write, a month rather than a few days? Time would no doubt produce a longer Orville Prescott review, but that it would produce a more constant inspiration is open to doubt. Richard Rovere mentioned somewhere recently the fact that he could find, today, great fascination in reading some casual article done by Edmund Wilson in 1924 for *Vanity Fair* or the *New Republic*. The longer essays Wilson has done in recent years on whatever topic engages his mind are literary works one could hardly expect regularly or even rarely in the *Times, Tribune,* or *Saturday Review.* Still, his earlier reviews are the sort of high possibility an editor would, or so one imagines, have in mind.

Nothing matters more than the kind of thing the editor would like if he could have his wish. Editorial wishes always partly come true. Does the editor of the *Times Book Review* really yearn for a superb writer like V. S. Pritchett, who *does* write almost weekly short pieces in the *New Statesman* with a week after week brilliance that astonishes everyone? Pritchett is just as good on "The James Dean Myth" or Ring Lardner as he is on the Russian novel. Is this the kind of thing our journals hope for, or is it a light little piece by, say, Elizabeth Janeway on "Caught between books"? It is typical of the editorial mind of the *Times* that it most frequently assigns Pritchett to write a casual, light London letter, work of insignificant journalism, which makes little use of his unique talents for writing book reviews.

In the end it is publicity that sells books and book reviews are only, at their most, the great toe of the giant. For some recurrent best sellers like Frances Parkinson Keyes and Frank Yerby the readers would no more ask for a good review before giving their approval and their money than a parent would insist upon public acceptance before giving his new baby a kiss. The book publishing and selling business is a very complicated one. Think of those publishers in businesslike pursuit of the erotic novel who would, we can be sure, have turned down *Lolita* as not the right kind of sex. It is easy enough, once the commercial success of a book is an established fact, to work out a convincing reason for the public's enthusiasm. But, before the fact has happened, the business is mysterious, chancy, unpredictable.

For instance, it has been estimated that the reviews in *Time* magazine have the largest number of readers, possibly nearly five million each week, and it has also been suggested that many publishers feel that the reviews in *Time* do not affect the sales of a book one way or another! In the face of this mystery, some publishers have concluded that *Time* readers, having learned *Time's* opinion of a book, feel that they have somehow already read the book, or if not quite that, if not read, at least taken it in, *experienced* it as a "fact of our time." They feel no more need to buy the thing itself than to go to Washington for a firsthand look at the latest works of the Republican Administration.

In a world like that of books where all is angular and unmanageable, there hardly seems to be any true need for these busy hands working to shape it all into a small, fat ball of weekly butter. The adaptable reviewer, the placid, superficial commentator might reasonably survive in local newspapers. But, for the great metropolitan publications, the unusual, the difficult, the lengthy, the intransigent, and above all, the *interesting*, should expect to find their audience.

CHAPTER 6

Who Needs No Introduction

Kingsley Amis

Public lecturing in America is the perfect vehicle for that rich compound of vanity and greed which makes up the literary character. I say "in America" not because Americans are particularly devoted to the two qualities mentioned, but because in Britain, at least, neither of them will get much of an outing at this form of sport: "I'm sorry so few people have turned up," one is likely to be told, "but our Mr. Snodgrass is also lecturing tonight—on French cathedrals—with lantern slides," and again, "I'm sorry the fee is so tiny, but we find if we charge admission nobody turns up at all."

In America, under I know not what system of inducement or threat, enough people will turn up to tickle even a writer's vanity, and greed is abundantly satisfied. Instead of having to wait a couple of months for five pounds, the common fate in England, one will probably be given the check before the audience has finished assembling, and if by any chance payment should be deferred until afterwards a good reason will be forthcoming: in Washington, I seemed to gather, a compatriot of mine got his little envelope after the preludial dinner and was never seen again.

Conscious of having had either one martini too few or one too many (a finer literary judgment is needed here than most of us possess) the lecturer makes his way to the podium and does his stuff, imperturbable and trying to sound improvisatory with his dog-eared script, uneasily alert for any face in the audience that even slightly recalls anybody who may have heard him deliver the identical talk last week in a different part of the town. This phobia is perhaps an integral part of the academic neurosis, likely to afflict all who have had to go through the motions, year after year, of sounding sprightly about *The Mill on the Floss* or *Martin Chuzzlewit* in front of undergraduate audiences; this year's lot look and behave so much like last year's lot that you can never quite convince yourself they are not the same lot. You need all your reasoning power for the reflection that nobody who has had to take two runs at the Freshman Novel Program (as it might be called in this country) is in danger of recognizing a supposed epigram however often it might be repeated.

But to abandon thoughts of home: our literary lecturer in America will meet, if he has been at all conscientious in preparing his remarks, a polite and attentive reception. The only man who ever made faces at me while I was holding forth turned out to be an official of Her Majesty's Government, which I was mildly denouncing at the time; they were mild faces too. Even that potentially dreadful aftermath, the question period, will generally slip harmlessly by without intervention from the aggressively well-informed or even the plain madman. Those well-tested life belts—asking for a 250-word question to be repeated, answering it with a monosyllable, breaking into uncontrollable laughter, etc.—can be left unused.

My one major error (the only one I know of, anyway) was committed when I gave an address at a well-known university in Philadelphia. Exhausted by the ceaseless search for wit, I had decided to abandon trying to tell jokes and deliver instead what was conceived as a hideously sophisticated joke in action: a long, humorless, pseudo-academic diatribe on the comic spirit recited absolutely deadpan by a supposed comic writer. As I recall—and one does not recall these things well, being concerned only to maintain continuity and aplomb, for all the world like somebody who has had too much to drink—as I recall it went down rather badly, except for a reference to vomiting which laid a single undergraduate in the aisle.

But retribution was swift: during the postludial party at the fraternity house somebody stole my script, which naturally, having a living to earn, I had been intending to run off elsewhere a few weeks later. I see now, of course, that the right way to interpret the felony was as (a) a blow against authority, to be welcomed as such, and (b) a second joke in action, a good deal more pointed and economical than my own. But I thought differently then.

It must have been vanity rather than greed which induced me to appear on a kind of public panel in a playhouse in New York: the topic, *Is There a Beat Generation?* My colleagues were Mr. James Wechsler, the editor of the New York *Post,* Mr. Ashley Montagu, the anthropologist, and Mr. Jack Kerouac, who as they say needs no introduction. At the preludial dinner it was explained that Mr. Kerouac was very nice, perfectly charming in fact, provided he was convinced that those present were on his side, felt sympathetic to him, in short *liked him.* I said I saw what was meant. Over in the theater we encountered Mr. Kerouac, conservatively attired in giant's-chessboard shirt, black jeans, and pigskin ankle boots. With hand on hip he piped to me, "Hallo, my dear" (I did need a haircut at the time, admittedly) and said to Mr. Montagu, "I saw you on the Jack Paar show. You didn't have anything new to say."

Having thus variously put the pair of us at our ease, he crossed to the backstage piano without giving us the chance to tell him how much we liked him. Then, seating himself at the instrument, he began a version of the dear old "Warsaw Concerto," but broke off every now and then to appear before the photographers. When he did this he weaved and bobbed rather as if about to start what we squares used to call jitterbugging. The "Warsaw Concerto" gave place at one stage to a boogie-woogie left hand, but was resumed after an interval when no boogie-woogie right hand was forthcoming.

Though Mr. Wechsler had still not arrived, some sort of gesture toward getting started was obviously called for. We trooped onto the stage and huge high-pitched enthusiasm arose from certain sections of the audience, a salute intended not for Mr. Montagu or me, I recognized sadly, but for Mr. Kerouac, who responded with more weaves, bobs, and a chimpanzee-shuffle or two. After some determinedly sedate remarks from the chair, Mr. Kerouac arose for what we all thought was understood to be a ten minute stint. During it, a stocky figure with overcoat thrown open entered at the back of the hall and made its way on to the stage; no beatnik anarch, as I had begun to fear, but Mr. Wechsler, in pretty good shape after a three-day editorial crisis and soon disabused of the idea that I was Mr. Montagu. Mr. Kerouac was talking about a swinging group of new American boys intent on life, forecasting the appointment of a beat Secretary of State, and saluting Humphrey Bogart, Laurel and Hardy, and Popeye as ancestral beats. Half an hour or so later he said he would read his poem on Harpo Marx. The texture of his discourse did not change. Throughout it seemed to illustrate the theme of the symposium rather than actually expound it.

Next there was me. Then there was Mr. Wechsler, who performed the considerable feat of advocating political commitment in terms that were both rational and free of cliché. Right at the start of it Mr. Kerouac muttered, "I can't stand this activist crap," and, wearing Mr. Wechsler's hat, began a somnambulistic pacing of the stage, occasionally breaking off to wave balletically at the photographers in the wings. He went on doing this while Mr. Montagu's ironies flew above the beat sections of the audience.

Finally there was "discussion." Mr. Kerouac accused Mr. Wechsler, very inaccurately, of having said a lot about what he didn't believe in and nothing about what he did believe in. Mr. Wechsler gamely responded with a capsule version of positive views. Mr. Kerouac leaned on the podium and said, "Admit it, Wechsler, you came here tonight determined to hate me." It was clear that none of us had managed to convince him that we liked him.

Disengaging myself from a 250-pound brunette who had leaped onto the stage to assure me that, contrary to my apparent belief, there was a beat generation, I followed the others out, reflecting that Mr. Kerouac's performance had acted as a useful supplement to his novels in demonstrating how little spontaneity has to do with talking off the top of the head. I also wondered, and still do, just what it is that people anywhere in the world get out of attending discussions or lectures by literary persons. For the majority, I imagine, one might as well speak in Choctaw; the visual appeal is what counts. For all his evident casualness, Mr. Kerouac was shrewd enough to have grasped that.

CHAPTER 7

Which Side of the Atlantic?

C. P. SNOW

Last spring, between stops in the United States, I found myself daydreaming about whether I would rather have been an American or an English writer. It was slightly more concrete than a daydream; for a number of writers on both sides of the Atlantic the choice exists. It doesn't for me; I am too much of a natural Whig. But the choice existed, of course, for Henry James, T. S. Eliot, and Auden. It might do so now for Amis or Wain on one side, or for Malamud or Podhoretz on the other.

The truth is, like it or not, that American and English writing still interweave as no other major literary cultures have ever done. For all the debating points made on both sides, for all the mutual irritation and envy, I doubt whether, in any strict sense, the two cultures are yet anything like completely separable.

That is why it is still open to a few English and American writers to choose which they are going to be. To opt for the other culture requires, of course, certain specific kinds of temperament and talent. Plenty of non-serious English writers have become Americans out of crude self-interest, but that is no more interesting than if they had gone to Switzerland to avoid income tax. I am thinking of people who want to make the most of their talent, and who are tough and confident enough to believe that the other side of the

Anglo-American culture may be a more encouraging climate than their own. They may be right, as James and Eliot demonstrably were. But, apart from romantic myth-making about the other country—which Americans still go in for about us, which young English writers increasingly do about you, and which in itself can be an origin for some kinds of art, as it was for part of James's—apart from that, the balance of advantage between being an English or American writer seems to me surprisingly even. There are plenty of general arguments both ways, but I believe there is only one of them that could reasonably decide anyone's choice.

It wouldn't affect a contemporary Henry James in reverse, for instance, that Americans have less feeling for the realistic novel than we have. We have to accept the case, put forward by Harry Levin in *The Power of Blackness* with his usual acuteness and command, that in the novel the Americans—for example, Hawthorne, Melville, Faulkner—have been led to produce works of the "extreme" imagination. Richard Chase has independently come to a very similar conclusion in *The American Tradition*. Either symbolism or naturalism, but not realism—that has been the American drift. It makes sense; it fits American social patterns. It has made American critics very uncertain of themselves in dealing with a writer like James Gould Cozzens. But it wouldn't prevent a realistic novelist of enough authority forcing himself into American consideration these next ten years; he would have to be pretty good, but if he were, he would change the climate quite a lot.

Then the language—American-English *vs.* English-English. Just as Americans are absurdly humble about whole domains of their literary equipment, the weight of their scholarship, the width and depth and intellectual sophistication of their best criticism, for example, so it is the fashion for Englishmen to prostrate themselves about the language, to speak as though having used the language for a good many hundred years was a fatal disqualification against ever using it again. A lot of English writers are so dazzled by the vernacular crackle of American-English that they don't hear other things. They don't hear—what worries a good many Americans when they get to work on discursive prose—that in a good many ways American-English is a significantly more abstract language than ours is. We say: "I want to book a seat." You say: "I want to make a reservation." That is part of common speech and works itself into the discursive prose. There is a great richness, sparkle, and invention in many of the American vernaculars, but the thought frame is often not as direct as in English-English. For a writer's purposes, the gains and loses linguistically just about cancel out.

There is another argument, far more substantial, that, if it were clear-cut, would certainly tip the choice. Even though it is not clear-cut, it is near enough the bone to inhibit contemporary Americans from doing a Henry James or a T. S. Eliot. I have talked to two gifted Americans who would, without any doubt at all, be great successes in literary England, They have thought about it; our culture would suit them; but they won't come. Somehow they couldn't do it; it would go against instinct and their sense of history. There is nothing mysterious about it; the balance of power has changed, and everyone feels in his bones that great literatures belong to countries at the peak of their power (as in fact they have done—Periclean Athens, Racine's France, nineteenth-century England) and sometimes to countries with the future in their eyes (Elizabethan England and nineteenth-century Russia).

If the U.S. were really sitting pretty, as unchallengeably at the peak of its power as England was, say, in 1830, with fifty invulnerable years as Top Nation ahead, then I should passionately envy American writers. But I do not see your position in those terms at all; I believe that essentially we are in the same boat. Of course you are richer and, as far as consumer goods go, likely to stay the richest country on earth. But that only exaggerates the true position, which is that the whole West, and the U.S. as the leader of the West, is a privileged enclave in the geo-social struggle, and that the real ferocity of advance, the dynamic social hope, lies in the great impoverished populations of the East just industrializing themselves, determined to have their share.

It is conceivable that this is going to be the century of the Common Man, but not as the phrase was originally intended. For the

Iowa farmer, the Los Angeles factory hand, are not in the least Common Men by the present world scale: they are privileged almost beyond belief. The genuine Common Men are the Chinese and Indian peasants; and reflective persons in the U.S. as well as in England are beginning to become aware that *their* condition is going to affect the fate of all mankind. I do not believe that the world is going to survive one-third privileged and two-thirds on the starvation line. Nor do thoughtful Americans believe it.

It is within the tension of that situation that we all sit and write. Not that we need give up our social hope. Given adequate foresight and nerve and good will, the problems can be solved. Nevertheless, the prospect takes a good deal of the buoyancy from American intellectuals—more, I sometimes think, than from us. Some of my American friends, such as Max Lerner, will quarrel with that last statement. Lerner thinks you are still more buoyant than we are. Within my experience, that does not seem to be the case. I don't feel in American writing today much of that gust of longing for the future that one finds in the nineteenth-century Russians, nor the wind of the continental spaces. As with us, American writers are adjusting themselves to a more difficult situation, to living in an advanced managerial society, more specialist, more pluralistic, harder to comprehend imaginatively than ours—while the rest of the world, apart from your poorer relations in England and in Western Europe, are struggling just to keep alive.

That seems to me the basic social insight which most American writers have come to live with. Even more than we, they are writing inside an advanced industrial society in its extreme form. The problems tend to be extreme, the solutions even more so. For instance, it is quite clear that in contemporary America, as in contemporary England, not many serious writers are going to earn a living out of their books alone. The potential rewards for one or two writers—the "jackpot"—are, of course, enormous, but most are never going to get them. Faulkner was middle-aged, Robert Frost old, before they drew a modest professional income from their creative writing. In an inflationary economy, this brutal fact about the career of letters is going to become a good deal more brutal.

The English and American responses to the fact are quite different. In England, which is a very small country, where anyone in the same profession is, at the worst, only one contact away from anyone else, we rely on a kind of private system of responsibility, and a little state help in the form of the BBC. If anyone of talent comes along, he will usually get a bit of help; the tradition of behaving like good uncles or aunts has descended in a peculiar line which includes Dickens, Trollope, Henry James, Bennett, Galsworthy, and the Sitwells; after the good uncles or aunts, the nexus, very intimate in England, of literary journalism-broadcasting-publishing will do something to keep the talented man afloat.

In the U.S. which is a very large country, and where even in New York distinguished literary figures show a cheerful unawareness of each other's existence, the solution seems to an Englishman to be out of comparison more drastic. It is nothing more nor less than to put the burden of literary patronage onto the universities. A great apparatus of visiting professorships, lectureships, fellowships, has sprung up which is providing a living, or the best part of a living, for an astonishing proportion of the best talents in the country. With about three exceptions, nearly every American writer who has been "heard of" in England, has had some help—and I mean help in the simple financial sense—from universities. A great many people whom we think of as professional writers are, or have been, permanent academics, or at least are regular teachers for half the year—Robert Penn Warren, Allen Tate, Trilling, John Crowe Ransom, O'Connor, Edel, Robie Macauley, Kazin, Mary McCarthy, Burke, Jarrell, Saul Bellow, Bourjaily, Stegner, Malamud, and so on, including nine out of every ten American writing names that come into an Englishman's head. Whereas their English analogues have usually not been near a university since they went down; and how many are regular academics? Amis, Iris Murdoch, J. I. M. Stewart—and then?

At present this is a dramatic difference between the two cultures. Perhaps, as with many American developments, it is a consequence of advanced industrial society, and in the long run we shall follow suit. At any rate, it is having many deep effects on American writing here and now. Writers are living in comfort and security in the U.S. as nowhere else. The wandering writer-scholars go from campus to campus, teaching a session at Iowa State, a session at Northwestern, a session at Stanford. They earn enough to get by, and a good deal more than their English equivalents. A very few will earn a lot of money in time from their books. A somewhat larger number will get *succès d'estime* and with that the kind of well-paid journalism which *succès d'estime* carries with it in the United States and which is unlike anything else in the world. The rest will have a more agreeable life than most writers. American universities, which have received so much lip from ignorant Englishmen that it makes me blush, are singularly attractive places to live in.

Yet American writers lose, as well as gain, by living in them. They are driven even more rapidly into the "Alexandrian situation." Universities, even American universities, more tolerant of creative writing than ours, are bound to be more critical than creative in their literary climate. It is right that they should be; but it isn't an easy, or altogether a healthy, climate to write in. It makes it harder for a man to write simply—not to disguise, by artificial irony or group mannerism, the solemnity of the moment in which he stands. I know a bit about this, for much as I love Cambridge, England, I found it inhibiting to write there. I think there is a danger that the academic ties will tend to make American writing more convoluted, more packed with invented symbols and ironies, altogether more Alexandrian.

There are great merits on the other side. The amount of intellectual horsepower being pumped into American literary discourse must be as much as in the rest of the world put together. I find myself increasingly admiring, as I read or listen to such men as Trilling, Levin, Henry Nash Smith, their sheer intellectual appetite, their ability to bring to bear upon a literary *point d'appui* every kind of intellectual resource, sociological, psychological, historical. High-level American literary debate makes much of ours seem amateur and lightweight. This intellectual edge and training save you from some of our follies; I don't think Jacques Barzun, rightly concerned about your run-of-the-mill intellectual training (worse, on the whole, than ours), gives enough credit to your best. A good many Americans have talked to me, with sympathy and a trace of *Schadenfreude,* about the Colin Wilson phenomenon. That at least, they thought, could not have happened there. They were too polite to say it, but they had no doubt that, intellectually, they were harder to take in. (Though aesthetically you are sometimes easier to take in than we are.)

And also, in such a large and pluralist society, collective hypnotism can't operate as in a literary capital like London. In London one often knows months before a book is published either that it is damned in advance, or that it is going to become the fashionable rage. That happens with popular successes in New York, but almost not at all—it seems to me—with serious works. There are, of course, coteries in the U.S. But there are so many counter-influences that no coterie can do much to make a reputation.

That is admirable. In some ways, it is almost too admirable. I have occasionally found myself thinking that it is altogether too hard for an American writer to make a reputation. Who has one? one wonders, rather like the young Proust wondering who is really grand. I have often asked American literary friends who, under fifty, is really in a literary sense established. Salinger? Undergraduates' enthusiasm. McCullers? No head. McCarthy? No heart. How *does* an American writer make a reputation? Everyone agrees that reviews in New York don't even start to do the trick. The university quarterlies? No one can point to a reputation made that way. Has any American novelist since Faulkner won anything like general serious recognition? No one is sure. Probably not. Meanwhile the centers of literary opinion proliferate and divide; literary society, like all American society, is more pluralistic than the English can imagine. The new advanced guard, the Structural Linguists, round on the New Critics as amiable old pipe-smoking fuddy-duddies, just as the New Critics got to work on Georgian survivals thirty years ago.

Up to now, the score has been a little, but not decisively, in the American writers' favor. But there is one last general argument which, as I said earlier, might for some of us clinch the matter. I think, if I were choosing, it would be decisive, and would make me stay in England. It is nothing very subtle, but it is linked with the size and nature of the English and American societies. It is simply that in England we know our audience. In America the writers don't really know whom they are writing for, apart from their fellow writer-scholars. Of course, any writer in an ultimate sense writes for himself; but he writes for himself in the presence of an audience over his shoulder, so to speak. The presence, constitution, critical powers, and responsiveness of the audience will interact with what he writes. A writer is likely to reach his creative best if the audience is sufficiently like him, so that he can speak in his own tone of voice, and at the same time sufficiently diverse to drive him to find his own special kind of originality. Compared with American writers, we are very lucky in both respects. Any reading public is a tiny minority of the whole population; with us, in a much more homogeneous society than the American, that minority shares enough assumptions to be a good audience, and is also pleasingly wide-spaced. For the present at least, we have not left reading entirely to fellow professionals: and I have no doubt that that is very salutary for a literature.

It is the variety of experience of the audience that gives it its authority, and so strengthens the writer's confidence. For example, Mr. Macmillan, Mr. Butler, Mr. Gaitskell are all deeply read men, interested in contemporary work; so are a good sprinkling of other members of the House of Commons. That is also true of a surprisingly high proportion of top civil servants and miscellaneous administrative bosses; much less true of industrialists, though I once sat at a meeting by the side of an eminent banker who kept distracting my attention by wanting to discuss the German translation of *The Possessed*. So our audience scatters itself through society, quite wide and quite deep, from the powerful to the young students; it is bracing for a writer to be read by both, and we should all like to be. In

England, the society is so compact that we realize that this is happening: we know, almost in a personal sense, whom we are writing for. An American writer can't; he feels much more lost. Do your politicians, civil servants, schoolteachers read as ours do? If they do, it seems to me that your writers do not feel their response. This, I think, is the one great creative stimulus ours have, which is denied to yours.

CHAPTER 8

On the Teaching of Writing

ARCHIBALD MACLEISH

Everybody knows that "creative writing"—which means the use of words as material of art—can't be taught. Nevertheless hundreds of professors in hundreds of colleges go on teaching it. Which is absurd but not as absurd as it sounds.

Everybody knows, too, that you can't teach a horse to race but Kentucky is full of racing stables with neat oval tracks and miles of expensive, white-washed fencing which costs as much to maintain as a presentable professor. Even more.

There is one difference, of course. In Kentucky they begin with the horse's sire and dam whereas the professor of writing rarely breeds his own students and wouldn't know where to begin if he tried. Who would have picked that pair from the livery stable to beget and bear John Keats?

But otherwise the situation in Cambridge is much like the situation in Kentucky. You have to have a horse that can race before you can teach it racing. You have to have a writer who can write before you can teach him how.

Which means, of course, that you aren't really teaching in Cambridge. To teach you have to have a subject: Elementary German or Physics A or The Novel Since Henry James. But there is no subject in "creative writing": there is merely an object: that boy (that horse).

I say *that* boy because there isn't apt to be more than one in a year or maybe in five or even ten. Indeed a man would be spectacularly lucky, even by Kentucky standards, to have one distinct and distinguishable writer of real power in a professional lifetime.

There are those, I know, who have tried to concoct a subject for "creative writing" courses by combining the best elements of the best writers in a kind of appetizer paste, a *mélange adultère de tous,* which their students are expected to consume. The young critics who make up the majority of any college writing course—the lads who have mistaken an interest in writing for writing itself—will thrive on such a diet but the young writers, if there are any, will gag on the surfeit. They know instinctively that there is no such thing as Best Writing. There are merely a number of different writers writing well and the successes of one would be the failures of another. You can't borrow and you can't mix. If anyone had tried to solve D. H. Lawrence's writing problems by teaching him Flaubert's solutions there would have been a suicide in the family attic, or more likely a murder in the local school. Exposition has rules and can be taught, as generations of British state papers demonstrate. The "art of writing" has graces and can be taught as armies of belletrists prove. But writing *as* an art cannot be taught because writing as an art is the unique achievement of *an* artist. Which is to say, of one unique and different man solving his unique and different problems for himself. When a student tells me that I haven't taught him *how,* I take it as a compliment—but not to him.

I am not saying, of course, that a young writer should not read. He should read his head off. But he should do his reading for himself, following the leads that are meaningful for him, not for someone else, and least of all for an odder professor-writer who did his own essential reading a generation ago and by a different light. To do an older writer's reading over again in a time like ours is to submit to that process, already so destructive in our fashion-following supercivilization, by which everything is turned into a vogue—even art which should be the great destroyer of all fashions, not their pimp. Everyone reads James. Then everyone reads Joyce. Then everyone switches to Eliot, to Proust, to Kafka—to the Communists in one decade—to the homosexuals in another—until the new writing begins to sound like the advertising patter in the smart magazines which echoes the changing chatter of the chic. It sometimes seems as though only Robert Frost were old enough and cantankerous enough and magnificent enough to be himself and remain himself and thus be disrespectfully and entirely new in this age of stylish novelties.

A real writer learns from earlier writers the way a boy learns from an apple orchard—by stealing what he has a taste for and can carry off. He will imitate his elders as every good writer has since the world began—even an original, even a Rimbaud—but the hunger and the pants pocket will be his own. Some of his apples will make him sick, but it will be *his* sickness. Others will shape his hand for life—because *he* picked them. When I set myself, after college and after law school, to try to find my way to a place where I could begin, I taught myself Italian enough to read *The Divine Comedy* because Tom Eliot had read it to his great profit and because I was—as I remain—his devoted admirer. It did me, I am sure, no harm. But neither did it do me Eliot's good, for it was not my need that took me to it.

The truth is that the whole situation in a writing course is a reversal of the usual academic pattern. Not only is there no subject, there is no content either. Or, more precisely, the content is the work produced by students in the course. And the relation of the teacher to his students is thus the opposite of the relation one would expect to find. Ordinarily it is the teacher who knows, the student who learns. Here it is the student who knows, or should, and the teacher who learns or tries to. The student writes. The teacher reads. And the object of the teacher's reading is to learn if he can how closely the knowing of the words approximates the knowing of their writer. It may be less. It may be far, far more, for such is the nature of the struggle between a writer and the obdurate material of words in which he works. But whether less or more, the only question the man who undertakes to teach can ask, is the question of the adequacy of the writing to its own intent. As a writer himself he may call it "good" or "bad." As a man he may have his human opinion of the mind which conceived it. But as a teacher of writing it is not his task to tell his students what they should try to write or to judge their work by the standards he would apply to his own or his betters.'

A student's poem does not fail because it is not Yeats's "Byzantium" or even "Sailing to . . ." It fails only if it is not itself. And the labor of the reader who calls himself teacher is the difficult labor of discerning, if he can, what "itself" would be. For only then can he bring his own experience and skill to bear upon it. Only then can he say to the student across the corner of his desk: "Well, if *I* had tried to write this poem . . ."

The real relationship, in other words—the only relationship in which anything in this paradoxical undertaking can be accomplished—is a relationship between two writers. Which is why it is essential that at least one writer should enroll in a writing course if it is to get anywhere. The problems which arise, young as the students are, are problems all writers face, whatever their age or experience. They are problems which cannot be discussed in a class, any more than in a bar in Paris, without a text to relate them to, and a writer's human experience to give them perspective. And they involve, as such problems always do involve, a writer's conception of the world: a conception different in every way from a critic's or a scholar's because a writer never gets *outside.* He works as Tolstoy works in *Anna Karenina*—at Levin's heart and Kitty's and Anna's. Techniques without works are as empty to a practicing writer as faith without works to a practicing clergyman: only amateurs would waste time talking about them.

But difficult as it is to describe the relationships of a writing course, it is even more difficult to justify one, either from the point of view of the student who takes it or from the point of view of the college which pays for it. (I defer, for a moment, the point of view of the poor devil of a poet or a novelist who tries to do the teaching.) Why, if all there is is a couple of writers, should any young writer send himself to a college writing course instead of to a park bench in Washington Square or a jazz session in San Francisco or any other spot where he might find an older writer willing to help him to help himself? And why, even with academic salaries what they are, should a college pay for the ten or twelve necessary hours of a professor's time every week if only one student a year or one student every five is going to profit?

I don't know the answer to the second question. You could probably justify a course in commercial fiction from the purely budgetary point of view if enough of its graduates sold stories to magazines with commercial prestige, but there is no way of adding up the justifications of a course devoted to the art of writing. Undoubtedly it is helpful to a college to be able to list a respectable number of writers as graduates but the trouble is that not all the proven writers come out of the writing courses. Harvard's poets from Robinson through Frost and Stevens to Aiken and Eliot and Cummings constitute an unequaled galaxy but I have never heard it said that any of them got their start in a writing course.

What justification there is must be academic rather than economic and there too one runs into trouble. One can argue that it is desirable to dilute the critical and scholarly atmosphere of a college community with a few artists but you won't get all the critics and scholars to agree. And if you remark that a good writing course will at least prevent English from becoming a dead language you might as well eat your lunches somewhere else than the faculty club. The plain truth is that these courses are eleemosynary enterprises so far as the college budget is concerned—opportunities provided to a small minority of students to investigate their artistic possibilities at the college's expense. The students who take them should be grateful. Sometimes, improbably enough, they are.

As for the first question, however, the answer is obvious. The young writer who graduates straight from high school into San Francisco, or wherever the people who used to congregate in Paris now hang out, in the innocent hope that he will thus combine his initiation into art with his initiation into life, is deluding himself. If we are to judge by its works there can scarcely be a worse place to get admitted to life than San Francisco. In comparison a great university or even a competent college is liveliness itself. There are more people of more kinds in a college than in a cult—particularly a cult in which Bohemianism itself is stereotyped and you can't even be a bum without bad liquor, boring sexuality, and the regulation beard. Indeed the American university—the American university I know best in any case—is almost the only place left in America where the infinite variety of the kind of life a writer wants to live can still be found.

In addition to which there is the highly pertinent fact that universities and colleges have books. Life is not all on the sidewalks or even in the bedrooms. The nine-tenths of it a writer needs under him to keep the rest afloat is in the books in which other men have put their living down. And there is one other consideration which bears upon those long conversations with older and sympathetic writers of which the young so understandably dream: most of the older writers are now employed by universities and colleges and the rest put limits on the number of young strangers they will entertain. Also the rest aren't as constantly available as the prisoners of the academic offices. They have a way of traveling to Africa or Spain.

As for the point of view of the poor devil who does the teaching, it can be given as briefly and simply as the annals of the poor. The rewards depend on the students. If they are uninteresting he will be bored to death. If they are exciting there will not be hours enough in the week. But it is not as simple as that, either. For if the students are dull the fault is his whereas if they are good *they* get the credit.

Mine have been good more often than I deserved.

CHAPTER 9

The Writer and Hollywood

BUDD SCHULBERG

Fifteen years ago when Elia Kazan arrived in Hollywood to direct his first motion picture he was initiated into the mysteries of the Midday Meal in the Big Studio Commissary. It was there he learned his first Hollywood lesson. What can a neophyte film director educated in the Broadway theater learn about his trade merely by having lunch? In Hollywood, status-happy capital of our Machine-age Art, lunch in a major studio is—or shall we use the optimistic *was?*—a revealing lesson in craft-caste.

At the conspicuous center tables were the grease-paint gods and goddesses of this celluloid Olympus, the marquee NAMES, surrounded by agents, publicity men, hairdressers and make-up men, stand-ins, relatives, columnists, cronies, court jesters, and the rest of the adoring entourage. At other choice tables were A directors with their staffs, and assistant producers and supervisors with theirs (top producers lived a life apart in their private dining-room). Other prominent tables were presided over by department heads (sound, cutting, etc.) and those lords of technicians, the cameramen, properly called directors of photography, with their chief assistants, the camera operators, the gaffers (bosses of the lighting crews) and the other vital members of the sixty-to eighty-man production team required for the making of a picture.

Finally there was, as Kazan describes it, ". . . a sorry group at a remote table. Their isolation was so evident that it seemed planned. There was no mixing with this group, no tablehopping to their table. . . . The writers . . ."

Kazan's first film was to be *A Tree Grows In Brooklyn,* written for the screen by Tess Slesinger, one of the few exciting new writers of prose in the 1930's. But in all his nine months of preparing, shooting, and processing his picture, he was never to meet Miss Slesinger. Undoubtedly she had long since been taken off the payroll, a hired hand doing piecework which could be used, ignored, changed, rewritten, or combined with the work of other writers as the producer willed or whimmed.

The invisibility of the screen writer came as a shock to Kazan, for his work in the theater had conditioned him to think of the writer as a man of dignity and pride—O'Neill and Robert Sherwood and Thornton Wilder and Clifford Odets, men who approached their plays as intensely personal statements. For better or worse it was *theirs,* for the director to interpret, perhaps even to embellish, but surely never to tamper with or change without their close collaboration and approval.

The shock of Kazan's recognition of the molelike status of the writer in Hollywood was something I had sensed all through my years of growing up in Hollywood. Yes, I had lived through it but I had never learned to live with it. In the early thirties when screen actors could no longer express themselves by a moody stare or the flutter of hand or eyelid but had to *talk,* an SOS was beamed to the East, a hurry-up call for what was then described as *real* writers, to distinguish them from the continuity boys, the gagmen, the idea-men, and the rest of the colorful if somewhat illiterate silent contingent. To the major studios, including one captained by my father, came novelists, playwrights, short-story writers, poets—a number of them of the first rank, some of them with Pulitzer Prizes, a few of them even more gifted than the prize-winners. I call up at random: Dorothy Parker and Samuel Hoffenstein, F. Scott Fitzgerald and William Faulkner, S. J. Perelman and John Van Druten,

John O'Hara and Edwin Justus Mayer, James Cain and Nathanael West, William Saroyan and Robert Benchley. These are just a few of the hired hands I bumped into out there. I used to look around at the dull stucco bungalows of the Garden of Allah and wonder if there ever had been such an assembly of literary lights all on the same small hotel register at the same time?

Yet, meshed into the Big Studio assembly-line system, almost none of these genuine writers produced anything genuine, anything memorable, anything by themselves and of themselves. Nathanael West had a pictorial mind and a Rimbaud sense of savage imagery. Oh what a film he might have written! But he used to go duck shooting from Friday to Monday and labor at workaday scripts for rent money the rest of the week. Scott Fitzgerald tried hard to adjust his undoctrinaire social consciousness and his Middle West romantic realism to the Hollywood demands; he broke his heart at MGM and his health came tumbling after. Eddie Mayer was on salary for the best of them year after year and there was literate wit in the dialogue but nowhere the richness of language and wit as character demonstrated in his Broadway successes like *Children of Darkness* and *The Fire Brand*. Perelman, O'Hara, Faulkner, all of them were summoned, all of them were paid the finest salaries in the history of hirelings, and not one of these distinctly identifiable voices could be heard above the insistent general hum of the dream factories.

Working as a junior-writer in this same period (a junior-writer being something that gets paid $75 to $300 per week, sort of a combination utility outfielder and batboy), I put in a frustrated apprenticeship writing scenes that somehow were sandwiched into other writers' scripts, or full shooting scripts that were never read, or screen plays which would be rewritten by teams of competent drones until the film that finally emerged was a three-headed-monster that startled me by occasionally speaking one of my lines or play-acting a whole intact chunk hacked out of one of my scenes.

Meanwhile a disquieting thing was happening to me—at least in terms of living in dishonorable harmony with what was then the Hollywood hegemony: I was beginning to find myself as a writer, as a pride-in-my-own-voice, do-it-myself writer. I listened to the bitter anti-producer, anti-Hollywood jokes of the Broadway playwrights and reputable novelists who had just signed their contracts for $50,000 or $75,000 a year. When they had enough cabbage in the bank (I would hear them dream and boast over the third martini, the fifth highball) back to the maple-shadowed New England farmhouse they would go; ah then they would write as their own men once again.

Fortunately for me I was still twenty-five. Youth is equipped with a built-in lie detector. Listening to these fine, sensitive, ruined men, I felt an uncontrollable desire to Go East, Young Man. I went, I wrote, I published, I luxuriated in the freedom of seeing every word remain exactly as I had put it down; every comma, if I wanted to be difficult about it. The last redoubt of individual enterprise, I called the novel. I had been pretty well paid for my screen-writing apprenticeship. I had hobnobbed with Parker and O'Hara, enjoyed long, wet lunches at Romanoff's, and gone to the big parties around the illuminated swimming pools. Yet when I found myself sitting at a writing table in the unglamorous East I felt the exhilaration of a runaway slave safely emerging at the northern end of the underground railroad.

For the next fifteen years, with four years canceled out by war, I devoted myself to fiction. But while I thought of myself as having broken successfully with Big Studio Hollywood, I discovered, from the perspective of a Pennsylvania farm, that the film, the composite art of the motion picture could not be so easily or glibly adjured. When, on those rare occasions it was good, it was so very very good that I often wondered if it was not still the most unfairly underrated and neglected of the arts. The great films lived on in my mind and took their place with the books and plays that moved me, excited my emotions, stretched my mind, disarranged me, and put me back together a little better or at least a little different than I had been before. The best of the Chaplin films had that power. And the wonderful old Jannings films. And comparable to the better books or plays of their year were such pictures as *The Informer,*

Grand Illusion, Citizen Kane, The Best Years of Our Lives, Open City, Brief Encounter, Rashomon, The Lost Weekend, The Bicycle Thief, The Treasure of the Sierra Madre. Such pictures as these, and a score of others, make us wonder if there is any story, any character, any mood, any theme, any truth that cannot be handled in depth on the motion picture screen.

If mediocrity seemed to be the major muse of the movies, if most pictures were turned out as mechanically as newspapers were rolled off their presses, and as quickly tossed aside and forgotten, it was not to be blamed on the shortcomings of the medium, as many of the middlebrows and even some of the highbrows claimed. The fault lay in a system of production that was the logical expression of American commerce in a period when the average family went to the movies—*any movies*—two or three times a week, and each of the seven major studios was grinding out fifty to sixty pictures a year. In all of Hollywood combined, feature-length pictures were being cranked off at the Detroit-precision rate of more than one a day. Rather than be surprised that there weren't more good ones, it is surprising that there were any good ones at all. What Hollywood managed to do—with those always notable exceptions—was to gear itself to a rather high level of mechanical efficiency. Inevitably some 375 of the 400 films a year would be standard product, slick, smooth, polished to a high professional gloss, and about as full of real life as the box of popcorn sold with the show.

In this popcorn, mass-production era, no wonder writers were tucked away in dark corners, or hired and fired out of hand like the itinerant odd-job men they were. The punishment fits the crime; the small-cog writer was fitted into the Frankenstein monster of the arts, the Boy-Meets-Girl Machine. In fact the screen writer reminded me of Charlie Chaplin's little man clutched to the mechanical bosom of the Modern Times machine. Trapped inside the inexorable mechanism was an individual, a man of nerves and feelings and dreams and convictions, crying, "Let me out! Let me out!"

Once in a great while the cries were answered. A writer like Dudley Nichols (*The Informer, Stage Coach, The Long Voyage Home*) would find his John Ford. A director-writer combination like Frank Capra–Robert Riskin would do their good *Deeds*. A pioneer visionary like King Vidor would sandwich an eccentric film of arresting self-expression between his more conventional big-budget assignments. Like Charlie's lonely, life-tossed, little poet-tramp, there were a few brave spirits who saw the motion picture for what it really is, the great common denominator of the arts, as treasured in Bangkok and São Paulo as it is on Times Square; the great global river of the arts fed by the tributaries of graphic art, dramatic writing, music, pantomime, and the editorial blending and counterpointing of all these separate elements which is the special contribution of the only art form conceived in the twentieth century.

While men like Dudley Nichols were urging their colleagues to shoulder their responsibilities and not degrade their talents by writing meaningless entertainments, I was working in the East in the conviction that I had turned my back on film writing for ever and that my old friend Dudley was crying in a klieg light wilderness. Hollywood, it seemed to me—in terms of any real creative life—had become a victim of its own prosperity. If Jeanette MacDonald-Nelson Eddy nonsensicals were the mass audience's idea of what was good and beautiful, why mess around with a character study of a homely middle-aged lump floundering in the net of Irish rebellion? If it is Betty Grable's legs that fill those seventeen thousand theaters, why fuss with Faulkner or O'Neill, or break new ground with an examination of racial prejudice (*Crossfire*) or a humanizing study of a third-rate prize fighter (*The Set-up*)? In fact when the artistic shortcomings of one of the Grable offerings was pointed out to a certain film executive, he came back with this industrial wisdom: "I only wish I had twenty-five Betty Grable pictures to sell this year."

And another leader of "the industry" (as the American motion picture business is always called), in charge of selling his company's product, looked back over the good old days of the 1940's and sighed, "Those were the days when this business was a pleasure. I didn't even have to look at our lousy pictures before I went out and sold them. Exhibitors bought our trade mark. They had faith in our product."

Between those two statements stretches a fifteen-year period in which Hollywood's bullmarket, Grable-Gable economy came crashing down. For those of us who had seen Hollywood grow from fly-by-night independent production in improvised barns to teeming, self-sufficient factory-cities like MGM or Twentieth Century-Fox, it was a historic and thought-provoking occasion. Mighty MGM, where a dozen mammoth sound stages had been in hectic and simultaneous use, had slowed to a standstill. For the first time in a quarter of a century, the streets of the vast studios were empty. The vast sound stages lay dead, side by side, like a school of beached whales. The machine-gods had lost the magic lamps that had given them the power of mechanical perfection.

The panic-swollen clouds of uncertainty had begun to cast their long, dark shadows over the Golden Valley of the Sure Thing. What had brought the monarchs of the mass audience to this dark hour?

Well, first came a government order prohibiting block booking. In other words, no more bulk selling of the good, the average, the indifferent, and the downright lousy. Every picture was forced to go it on its own, which placed an inefficient but sometimes inspiring emphasis on individual effort.

In the second place, there was a new rival machine-monster, television. People could sit home in their slippers, suck on their beer cans or their baby bottles, and enjoy playlets no worse, or at least not much worse, than they were getting on four out of five nights at their movie theaters. The old movie habit, a significant twentieth-century American institution that had made a dozen enterprising and farsighted immigrants multi-rich and self-satisfied, was dead. "When the people go out of the house now they are shopping for what they want to see," a lost last-tycoon said to me with a sad shake of his puzzled head.

And as if this wasn't trouble enough, the public was beginning to show some stirrings of maturity. No more twelve-year-old minds. The public seemed to be reaching at least an enlightened stage of adolescence. They knew storks had nothing to do with it and they were receptive to the idea that man's reproductive drives provoked tensions, conflicts, disorders, early and late sorrows, and both sad and happy endings that were just as dramatically satisfying as the fairy-tale romances that had monopolized their entertainment for the first fifty years.

One indication of this new dawn was Kazan's coming out to my farm half-a-dozen years ago to talk to me about writing a picture for him. I told him why I had burned my Hollywood bridges, and he—still thinking in terms of the dramatist's need and right to identify himself with his material—urged me to write on a subject that attracted us both—the corruption of the harbor of New York—with the same sense of freedom I would have if I were writing it as a book (as I had planned to do). With the support of an independent producer (no major studio being willing to underwrite what was considered an unpalatable and uncommercial subject) we conceived of *On the Waterfront* as a film we would do together.

"One of the things I've done, against all business advice, is to upset the traditional balance and make the writer more important than the stars," Kazan wrote of this experience. "I don't think it's a mistake. I think we have a wonderful chance right now. The breakdown of the old standardized picture-making has made room for creative people. It is a boon to anyone who has something personal and strong to say. For art is nothing if it is not personal. It can't be homogenized. By its nature, it must disturb, stir up, enlighten, and offend."

In this spirit, no longer an invisible man, encouraged to be on the set every day rather than chased off as an intruder as I had been in those junior-writer-assembly-line days, I was able to project myself into *The Waterfront*. If the logic of the work seemed to demand that a scene be changed I was there to do it. If there were lines to add or delete—as required by the staging or the actor's originality or the exigencies of shooting on the actual docks and in the bars and tenements of Hoboken, I was on the set to write the necessary lines or approve the eliminations. I couldn't truthfully say, as with a novel, for better or worse it's all mine; for a film—at its best—is a creative cooperative, in which the original conception of the author must fuse with that of the director, the producer, the leading players, and finally the film editor and composer. Still, with *Waterfront,* and teaming with Kazan again on *A Face in the Crowd,* I was able to retain a pride of authorship. I saw my ideas and my characters brought to the screen as faithfully as Kazan and our actors could interpret and develop them.

To be sure, this rather unprecedented elevation of the screen playwright's status does not assure artistic and commercial triumph. I often think of film-making as a horse race in which teams of three or four or five horses must run together. If they run at all it is rather remarkable. If they run as well as they can, manage not to trip each other up, and cross the finish line together, it is a not-so-small miracle. This may explain why the most gifted of film-makers, Ford, Stevens, Huston, Kazan, may achieve only three or four truly memorable films in a lifetime of hard work.

Rossellini and De Sica were towering neo-realists of Italy's post-war film renaissance, but it is a singular fact that they only towered when they worked in harness and harmony with a writer who shared, indeed inspired, their vision. De Sica's *Shoe Shine, The Bicycle Thief,* and *Umberto D* were done in collaboration with Cesare Zavattini. And although the fame and notoriety of Rossellini obscured the contributions of his colleagues, it was Federico Fellini (now celebrated as director-creator of *La Strada*), who wrote *Open City, Paisan,* and *The Miracle.* Two men sharing a single artistic vision? It sounds improbable, if not downright uncomfortable, and even faintly immoral, like two men trying to share a single bed.

In several years of working together Kazan and I talked, wrote long letters, pooled and mused and fused until we felt we were as close to eye-to-eye as two people with different sets of eyes can be. Even then there were inevitable differences. We wondered how Solomon would separate the delicate strands of artistic authority and decided that on the writing, while Kazan would deeply involve himself, I would have the last word. On the set, I would watch, weigh, suggest, contribute bits of business and impromptu dialogue, but here it was Kazan who finally had the yes or no. Most of the time, though, we worked out our problems without having to refer them to our personal Court of Appeals. An intense period of pre-production creative fellowship had conditioned us to a telepathic state where one could say, "What if . . . ?" and the other cut in, "Yes, I see what you mean. Let's see if it works."

The problem of the single-minded, two-headed vision is com-pounded when one recalls some of the criticisms of our *Face in the Crowd*—that it was excessive, that it shifted in style from realism to satire to burlesque, that the scales were tipped unfairly and inar-tistically against its demoniacal folk-hero-villain, and that Kazan and I were too close to each other and too consumed by mutual fascination with our material to provide the necessary check and balance of perspective. How to create together and still not surren-der one's identity? It is the complexity of any satisfactory answer to this question that has prompted me to grumble that a first-rate film is more difficult to achieve than either a good novel or a successful marriage.

Despite these hazards, the trend is in the direction of a new, wide-open kind of film-making, similar to the director-writer partner-ships that have created so many of the European films memorable for their originality and truthfulness. No longer do the big stu-dios grind out their fifty-sixty pictures a year. They are turning over the reins to scores of independent production companies, many of them, it must be admitted, built around stars for tax-dodging purposes, but a number of them headed by outstanding directors in search of creative independence. And the major studios have even come around to backing companies founded on the reputations and contributions of that once low-man-on-the-totem-pole, the writer. There is a Paddy Chayefsky (*Marty*) company, a Daniel Taradash (*From Here to Eternity*) company, a Joe Mankiewicz (*All About Eve*) company, a Carl Foreman (*High Noon*) company and, may Ran-dom House forgive me, even a Schulberg company. And beyond these, there are another dozen writers encouraged to write and pro-duce or direct their own work, in other words allowed to follow through from the first word to the final print. This is no insurance,

of course, against claptrap stories, cliché situations, faulty judgments, dishonest endings, in fact the whole glacier of mediocrity
that has so often in the past leveled off the creative peaks and flat-
tened everything to a pedestrian sameness. But if a *Citizen Kane,* a
Marty, a *La Strada* have anything in common it is a *signature.* They
may not be as perfect as a can of concentrated orange juice but they
have more personal flavor. They have been touched by human
hands, not always the cleanest, maybe not even the most skillful. I
would rather see an O'Neill play for all its excesses than the famil-
iarly clever well-made Broadway play, and I would rather read a
Faulkner novel for all its exasperatingly congealed wells of experience than a glib best-selling Metalious or even a righteously out-
pouring Leon Uris. Similarly I would rather see an uneven and
unresolved stab at life like *Baby Doll* than the latest cellophane-
wrapped standardized hit at the Music Hall.

But the chancy and exciting fact is that nobody can predict a
sure-fire hit any more. Sinatra and Grace Kelly in a romantic paral-
lel to the Monaco fairy tale? No go. Bill Holden and Sophia Loren in a
sea-going adventure with sexual overtones? Still no go. Then what
do the people want? Nobody quite knows. And the headmen in
the executive dining-rooms are the first to admit it. For the front
office it is a difficult period of adjustment. For the writer seriously
interested in motion pictures it is an unprecedented opportunity, a
new ball game. After twenty-five years of high-class serfdom, he's
being invited to come forward to the center tables. For the first time
in American film history the writer—that is if he is willing to fight
for his rights—is being given his head. Now, while the bonds of
censorship are loosening, and the film-going natives are restless for
something new, it is up to him to use it.

CHAPTER 10

The Lost Art of Writing for Television

VANCE BOURJAILY

When national television arrived in the United States a dozen years ago, it was, or should have been, a challenge to our writers without precedent in the history of human culture. Here was a stage to write for as large as the nation itself, with unparalleled reach into people's lives, with a good deal of money to spend, with great expanses of continuous time to be filled, and—above all—with the demand that artists invent it as a medium for art as successfully as scientists had developed it as a technical wonder.

Perhaps the challenge was too large and too explicit; whatever the reason, we seem, except in one brief period, to have faced it squarely with our backs; we can turn around now. The challenge is gone.

Television has developed a staggering number of bad ways of filling that national stage, reaching into those hundred million lives, using up the energy and time; it has even developed a few good ones. But for all the years of hours that have passed on its screens, it has not generated a dramatic literature worth more than this footnote of attention.

Yet there *were* pioneers who tried to create such a literature— Paddy Chayefsky, Robert Alan Aurthur, N. Richard Nash, Horton Foote, Rod Serling, Reginald Rose—others, perhaps, whose plays I did not see. I wrote television plays for a living but what television

I watched, I watched with my left eye. Thus, if you wish to name the guilty, you may name me first as representative of the writers from other fields who were indifferent—who would take television's fees but would not become seriously ambitious for themselves in the medium.

But others were guilty too. In the brief period in the early fifties which produced the beginnings of a worthwhile television literature, readers and intellectuals were prominent among the indifferent. They echoed the women's clubs in deploring the possible effect of all that eyestrain and inactivity on their children, and added that, as for themselves, they seldom turned on the set except to watch the fights.

I never heard literary people discussing such problems as the form which drama must take to be really suited to television; or taking sides on issues like the strengths and weaknesses of live as opposed to filmed plays; or joining the debate about the merits of New York, as opposed to those of Hollywood, as a production center.

The men who did discuss these matters were not literary intellectuals; they were the medium's own intellectuals, directly connected with it as writers or directors or actors or producers or advertising men. If there were also viewers who cared, and took a serious interest in these matters I did not meet them. I never, for example, met a man who had seen the television presentation of TV's most famous play, "Marty"; the people I heard debating its merits were talking about the movie.

Who else should be named as guilty? The pioneers themselves, for deserting the medium. Yet I excuse them more readily than I would the writers who never tried and the intellectual viewers who never watched. It is understandable that the important television dramatists work no more in a field which offers small scope for their ambitions, and which, in addition, does not pay very well. In the year or two when I was getting most of my earnings from television, an hour-long script paid $2,500; to have four such scripts assigned a year was above average. The name writers may have got slightly higher fees, and as many assignments as they wanted, but even so the payments were far below the forty or fifty thousand dollars they could earn from writing a pair of movie scripts in a year. They are writing movies now, and plays (not necessarily good ones), which is what they always meant to do. For a moment television seemed to offer them excitement, reputation, opportunity to be truly creative—a way might even have been found of perpetuating their work. This moment was soon over; when television offered merely less money for more work, of course they left.

Finally, there are the guilty always named in the standard indictment—the networks, the advertisers, the rating services, and the public. Let the indictment stand; it is all true and all, in some drab way, forgivable. The networks, as businesses in a business society, must be expected to look on quality programing only as a form of public relations unless it pays its way; the advertisers cannot be expected to use truth willingly to illustrate their ads; the rating services and the public must be acknowledged as eternal mirrors of one another, a bit warped, perhaps, toward a mutual image of idiocy, but on the whole more informative than not.

My point is that these villains of the standard indictment are what they always were; if there was a brief time when they were held in check by a creative force they did not want or understand, then it was our indifference—yours and mine—which deprived the genuine talent of the support it needed to withstand them.

To describe what television's creative period produced in the way of a body of generic literature, however small, we should exclude, to begin with, almost all television dramas made from stage plays. They are not really adaptations; they are only condensations, and are no more genuine works of television art than were those quaint, first efforts to achieve art in photography by costuming models and grouping them to resemble the figures in famous paintings.

Similarly we must exclude novels adapted as television plays. If they are slight enough in scope to have been previously shaken down for successful use on stage or screen (like "So Little Time" and "The Caine Mutiny Court Martial") then they can probably be further reduced for television. Neither of these was hard to watch when aired, but neither in any way approached art. Quite the opposite happens with television adaptations of more profound novels; the approach is so solemn, the plays are so portentously over-produced and over-cast—at the expense of adequate rehearsal or enough time and care spent on writing—that the result can only be tedious and artificial; for example last year's production of "The Bridge of San Luis Rey" held the viewer's attention only by a steady—and unrewarded—effort of his will.

Short stories have provided better source material for television plays because the dimensions of a one-hour television play are rather like those of a short story.

To be excluded also from consideration as TV literature is the half-hour show, and, for quite different reasons, most of the ninety-minute dramas.

The half-hour show is too brief, and is interrupted by a commercial too soon after it begins, to be anything but a hook, a gimmick, and a resolution. A couple of half-hour shows I wrote seemed to me no better than the rest—since there was no time to develop character, they required twice as much plot complication as an hour show. I can conceive of a half-hour script—a Chekhov story for example—focused on a single character, in which a remarkable actor might achieve dramatic force in a sustained performance. I have not, however, seen any such plays and can only imagine them.

As for the ninety-minute form, I am reluctant to dismiss it as fruitless. The best men went to those shows, if they didn't leave the field completely; I cannot believe, however, that they found there the freedom to produce, subject only to the supervision of their own artistic consciences, that they once had in the one-hour field.

But after all exclusions are made, television *did* create something—perhaps two or three dozen fifty-minute plays of genuine literary worth, whose excellence was uniquely suited to the medium and inseparable from it. These were, as I have said, more related to the short story than to any other literary form. They had a singleness of effect and mood which would have robbed of variety an extended work like a three-act play or movie. They had a unity of situation, and avoided complication in exploring it. They were, in effect, composed of three scenes—each constructed out of smaller episodes—miscalled "acts" in a fanciful attempt to equate commercial breaks with theater intermissions.

Like short stories, most of these plays explored, often in surprising depth, just one relationship—between members of a family, or a man and a woman; sometimes the focus was even restricted to an individual. They could be called plays only in that they were performed; they were like movies only in that they were projected.

For as plays they lacked, of course, the vitality of real flesh and voice on which the playwright relies to hold a silent audience, spellbound together in the dark, during long scenes. And they lacked, too, the movie's great resource of unlimited movement. A one-hour television play must be held to about five rather modest sets, though the use of tape may change this. The cast must be held down, generally to fewer than ten speaking parts for reasons both of space and costs.

The group of plays I am speaking of were not hampered by these restrictions; on the contrary their excellence was, in part, a product of them. For the limitations pushed the writers into using close examination as their basic technique, in the fashion of naturalism in fiction.

This is, of course, not an original observation. It is, rather, a proposition I heard discussed and found convincing in the days when television writers were enough interested in their field to theorize about it. They argued that the details of the narrative must be observed with meticulous realism, with the effect of a conversation overheard from the next room and seen through a hole in its wall. With the viewer thus identified with the screen, one could then through the use of close-ups build up toward a climax. This concept did not produce great dialogue, but it did produce some that was very moving.

This is not perhaps the only mode in which television drama can be artistically successful; it may have been merely the first area of exploration, but it was the only one, in my experience, in which any interesting work was done.

As a specimen, I would ask you to view, if you could, Chayefsky's "The Middle of the Night," a TV play which I prefer to the same author's "Marty." The fact that the same script, expanded for the stage, made rather a bad play, demonstrates to me that its excellence was generic. (I have not seen the movie version.)

"The Middle of the Night" concerns three people: a fragile, beautiful, and quite neurotic girl, a flower of the Bronx; an ugly, gentle, older man—her garment district employer—lonely and unable to believe that so valuable a creature can return his love; and finally the girl's physically-appealing estranged husband, who seems, in our stereotype of youth and good looks, to be a more appropriate lover for her. But the narrative proceeds to remove surface; a series of intimate scenes (girl and mother, girl and lover, girl and sister, girl and husband) reveal that the girl's real need is to be cherished as the older man would do. The play ends as it must: the girl and the middle-aged man will pool her fears and his loneliness in a kind of crippled marriage, which is scarcely a triumph but at least makes the best of things. Against the single, wistful mood of this story, Bronx life showed up on TV as a series of harsh ironies. Yet when it was blown up into a stage play, it resembled soap opera.

Wistfulness, of course, was not the only mood of the fine TV plays. There was a sardonic extravagance in much of Robert Alan Aurthur's work; a sure hand with character tensions in the work of Rod Serling; a memorable tenderness in the plays of Horton Foote.

Precisely how many plays like these were shown in the first years of television, I do not know; they were seen once, in most cases, and then discarded. There may have been writers as successful as those I cite whose work I didn't see, haven't heard of. Whatever their number, it is of them that the dramatic literature of television is composed.

I am not qualified to report in detail how these plays were nurtured, and how the form withered away. What follows will be impressions and opinions. I had some fifteen shows performed during about four years, but this was at the end of the era. Many men could give more complete and accurate accounts than mine—Fred

Coe or David Susskind or Robert Alan Aurthur to name three among many. But I doubt that any of them will, and of course I do not mean to associate them with my views.

The chief source of the kind of television play I have described was the Philco *Playhouse,* as organized, I believe, by Coe and produced on Sunday nights over NBC. (Fred Coe later went over to CBS, where he produced *Playhouse 90.*) My first script was for Philco, which was then being produced by Robert Alan Aurthur and Gordon Duff. There was much in the *Playhouse* which led an author to become quite serious about television, quite excited, quite ambitious. Duff and Aurthur seemed free to do precisely what they wanted, in that summer of 1955. I remember being much impressed when Aurthur said, in our first interview:

"We do fifty-two plays a year, and we know perfectly well they won't all be triumphs. We'd rather have our failures represent writers' experiments, things we risked, than do formula shows."

And later I believe it was Duff who said: "What we believe in basically is writers. If we can find them and keep them working, the plays will come."

A producer's freedom to take such attitudes is the essential condition, I am certain, for a writer to do creative work. One needs to know that the script will be submitted to the judgment of a man's true taste, not to artificial requirements. (I am not speaking here of taboos; there are taboos in every form, and while television's are more prevalent and sillier than most, they cannot smother art, nor can limitations of time and technique.) A limitation is an annoyance within which one can work. But a requirement is something different and poisonous—it formulates what a script *must* do. A writer and producer cannot work seriously toward drama, if a sponsor requires that regardless of subject the script must be inoffensive and uncritical, or if the test of achievement is how well it provides a synthetic excitement to compete with another network for the attention of the regular viewer—the attention, it is always assumed, of the dim-eyed and slow-witted, whom television struggles to win from comic books and low-grade movies.

Along with the freedom, the *Playhouse* as I knew it had another essential for creating good television plays: it had a strong editor in Robert Alan Aurthur. Live television is very largely a script editor's medium, just as the movies are chiefly a director's medium. A month may be spent on the preparation of the script—compared with ten days on its production; the editor's vision is an indispensable guide to structure and sequence for the writer. This at least was always true for me.

The *Playhouse* had other assets, equally important. It had access to an acting pool, concentrated in New York in the early fifties, since dispersed and reviled as "Actors' Studio types." From these players their directors could draw the kind of inward, understated, but cumulatively powerful performances which the naturalism of television requires.

My own rather tentative first script was submitted in the summer of 1955 when many of the best television writers were already moving out of the industry to write movies, plays, and novels. The producers scheduled it almost as soon as I had completed the first draft. This was only possible, of course, because of the shortage of experienced writers. But I was unaware of this. I was too excited. They brought me to New York to do the rewriting, put me in a hotel, and rented me a typewriter. Even before I finished the rewriting, I found myself involved in the excitement of the production; I talked to the set man, was consulted on casting, helped choose the music. It was the policy at the *Playhouse,* and a fine teaching instrument for the writer, whether he contributed much or not, to involve him in the realization of his play at every possible point; one went to rehearsals, ate lunch daily with the cast, argued cuts and readings with the director—it was his show now—the producers were working on their next one.

I remember the pre-show tension at dress rehearsal, and the loneliness of sitting away from my friends in the cast, in a viewing room waiting for them to begin, and the pleasure of seeing the producers come into the room to watch with me. There was a party afterward. . . .

I know of no show done in New York now in which the author participates in that way, nor would I want to today. The procedure, as I know it, now goes like this: the cast, writer, production staff, and representatives of the agency meet some ten days before performance. Copies of a corrected script are handed around for the cast to read. The reading is timed; everybody listens. At the end, a player may question some lines, then the cast leaves. The writer, editor, producer, director, and agency representative each suggest changes. They are noted by the writer, as they are agreed upon. He then goes off and makes all the cuts and changes as rapidly as possible; generally the reading ends at noon, and the writer's final work is done before five. He will then turn over the script and leave, hoping fervently to have nothing more to do with it; he will probably watch the play when it is aired, if he is not too busy, and he may grumble insincerely about changes made without consulting him; but in truth he is no more deeply affected than he once was when he used to glance through his newspaper feature story to see what the copy desk had done to it.

If there is a party after his play, he will not be at it, nor want to be, nor will the actors except perhaps the star, who may be required to meet the sponsors and their friends. The party is for these people, and their agency and network colleagues. And it ought to be; it was their show. But it was our show on Philco; we were all deeply involved for we were aiming at art.

A day or two after the first show, Aurthur approved an idea I had for a second, but he seemed worried; he suggested that I wait a few days before writing the outline, for the sponsor now had to see outlines before plays were commissioned. I then became aware that the *Playhouse,* and a number of the other good hour shows, were under attack. It had started during the summer, when a few weak shows by the undeveloped new crop of writers had made Aurthur and Duff vulnerable. Sponsors were snarling for more control, agencies for more of the budget to be spent on stars, networks threatening to sell the drama hours for other kinds of programing.

One of the most important critical voices, according to my strong impression at the time, came from a most unexpected place: it seemed to come from a man who represented himself as a champion of serious television drama, Jack Gould, the television critic of the *New York Times.* Since following Mr. Gould's writing more recently I am now less surprised, for he reflects an attitude common in television criticism: that serious drama somehow means *solemn* drama, or pretentious drama, or message plays on topical matters.

I don't know whether Mr. Gould coined the term, but it was in his columns in the summer of 1955 that I became aware that a curious word was being popularized and attached in a derogatory way every Sunday to the *Playhouse* and others like it. The word was "psychodrama." With it you could tar not only the writers' experiments that had failed that summer, which might have benefited from more precise criticism but, by implication, all their predecessors which were in fact the only fine plays television has created.

The crusade against psychodrama was joined jubilantly by *Variety* and all the other trade journals. Soon there was a behind-the-scenes demand that *Playhouse* commission a play glorifying that happy event, the Miss America contest. (Around this time an editor on another show boasted to me that they had *always* stressed real entertainment values to their writers as the first requirement; and Herb Gold, who was then looking into television writing, told me he had been asked to guarantee "happy plays about happy people with happy problems.")

"Psychodrama" or not, the delicately observed, honestly written, and meticulously performed plays of the early, naturalistic dramatists, as done by the Actors' Studio-influenced actors, were not solemn or pretentious; they were not often topical and, because they were concerned with reality, they were seldom happy.

In the new climate, I was not asked to start drafting that second play for the *Playhouse;* and I was not much surprised to hear that Duff and Aurthur had resigned rather than give up their freedom to produce as they wished. I was rather glad they had quit; I hadn't liked to think of them doing that play about Miss America.

In writing of the period that followed, I may be slighting some producing organizations. Yet my impression was that none was ever again as free as the *Playhouse* had been. *Studio One,* for example, continued to do ambitious things after the panic, though one editor told me candidly that sponsor approval was needed on outlines. In television a writer seldom knows more than the producing organization he is currently working for. He is in a group which gets assignments for a particular series, and there is no true free-lancing in the field.

The idea for the script may be the writer's; more often it is the producer's, or is arrived at in conference. The assignment is then made after the writer and editor have worked out an extremely careful outline. To write a complete script and hope to sell it is, as far as I know, an utter waste of time. The wheels do not turn that freely and what they have been turning out of late is not dramatic art.

To be sure, there are dramatic shows on television now. But, so far as I know, there is no television drama. Nor is there genuine television criticism. If there had been one eloquent critic, concerned with and able to recognize literature, who wrote regularly about television, he might have influenced its course. But genuine critical minds showed no interest in the medium.

Over the years television has shaped itself more in the image of the newspaper than the theater. To spend an entire day with the networks (there are those who do; and they count in the ratings) must be like reading an interminable newspaper, sometimes well-written and well-illustrated, sometimes badly. There are the news, the women's pages, the circulation contests; there are reports on, or excerpts from, culture and the arts, often excellently done by Sunday shows like *Omnibus* and *Camera Three;* there are the news-making shows, which are like press conferences, and live coverage of sporting events often better than the sports pages; how-to shows, perhaps an editorializing play, or a documentary which is like a feature story.

And always, there are the ads.

The editorializing plays, if they have nothing much in common with literature, can sometimes do nice bits of social service, just as journalistic crusading can. I once wrote a show, for example, about the plight of Korean War orphans and was pleased to hear that it had been responsible for clearing out an orphanage by stimulating adoption. But it was not literature, any more than was a well done reportorial play about the Nuremberg trials I saw on *Playhouse 90* recently.

Finally, in television as in newspapers, there are the comics. Newspaper comics, as has been often observed, are rarely meant to be funny; many of them seem directly derived from soap opera. Many others are Westerns, adventure, or detective strips. A few are funny; there is sometimes one for children.

The television counterparts for comics, when one thinks of it this way, are all too evident; they include all the entertainment shows on the air. But if our newspapers allotted space by a rating system a thirty-page issue would contain two pages of news and twenty-eight of comics.

There are some expertly produced comic strips; by the same token some entertainment shows in television just now are slickly written, engagingly acted, and produced with a crisply professional finish. My particular favorites in this category are *Maverick* and *Alfred Hitchcock Presents*, and I honor one for children, *Captain Kangaroo*. *Maverick*, in particular, is remarkable—the only one of the adult westerns which avoids their synthetic set of tolerance symbols (Indian equals Negro; young gunfighter equals juvenile delinquent) and value symbols (woman equals culture; frontier doctor equals wisdom).

Along with all these other newspaper-like aspects of television, there are the special feature sections: the spectaculars, shows of the month and so on. Like newspaper special sections, they are bait to lure the chary advertiser in, or the small advertiser to go big. When successful, the spectaculars are triumphs of production rather than creation. One does not feel the presence, much less the dominance, of an individual writing intelligence. Indeed it has been years since

I saw a play on the screen with any vision of what the art of television drama might be.

For a return of this vision, I can conceive two hopes. One is pay television which would have to win, not mesmerize willing audiences.* This might force all entertainment shows to reach the level of *Maverick,* in order to survive. The longer plays, since their object would be gain, rather than institutional advertising and public relations, might have less pretension and more sting; they could risk being offensive, but not tedious; they would be at the minimum, show-business instead of ad-business. This is not necessarily a condition for producing art, but it is at least a step closer to it.

Pay television, then, might become a medium as good as the movies which, generally speaking, is not terribly good; yet the movies have, from time to time, produced works of art, and there are "art" theater circuits on which these works play and replay. Perhaps we could develop a pay TV equivalent of the "art" theater circuit which would sustain itself largely on re-runs; this would solve a basic writer's problem for it is hard to be seriously ambitious for a piece of work which will disappear after one performance.

And to speak of this is to bring up a less visionary notion, and one to which the networks are welcome if they wish to try it. It is very practical. They will find in their storerooms reel after reel of kinescopes of hour-long plays, performed over the years on the various "anthology shows"; *e.g.,* such shows as *Philco, Studio I, Kraft Theater, Matinee Theater.* They could easily establish an evening and a time, a late and inexpensive time now occupied by old movies, for showing, perhaps once a week, an old television play. They could, if they would, put into repertory what drama television has managed

---

* Another possibility was outlined by John Fischer in *Harper's* last August. He proposed (1) that the government rent air channels to TV and radio stations for a modest percentage of their earnings and (2) create with the proceeds an independent National Broadcasting Authority to produce worthy public-service programs—including good theater—which would be presented on the major networks. But unfortunately this plan is a long way from realization.

to develop. It would cost very little; it would interest viewers a good deal more than most of the movies shown; it might even attract sponsorship.

And it might afford a few youngsters, who will be writers some day, examples from which to develop their own visions of a television drama. I do not think embryo writers watching the medium now have any such feeling for the possibilities of writing for TV.

If such future writers are among us something else ought to be done to develop them—but this is so impractical a dream that I will not try to suggest how it might be implemented. They ought to be given a chance to work with regular producing groups (like the Philco *Playhouse*? Perhaps, and like the Provincetown Players, which produced O'Neill, and the Group Theater, which produced Odets).

The interaction of writer and actor, writer and director, writer and producer is what makes playwrights. Why could not such a company be set up (not necessarily in New York; possibly where costs are lower) and charged with creating and performing a television play every week? They would have to be made responsible to nothing but their mutual vision and their audience—I mean *their* audience, not the audience—and financed by any means at all: sponsorship, pay TV, foundation, it doesn't matter. Given a life, not merely a trial, I am convinced that out of such a situation television drama of stature would once again be written in our land.

CHAPTER II

How and Why I Write the
Costume Novel

FRANK YERBY

Editors, writers, and students sometimes ask me how to write "best-selling novels" but I am always forced to disappoint them. If I knew how, I should most certainly turn one out every year. The fact is I try and sometimes—rarely—I succeed, more often, I come reasonably close; occasionally I fail.

However, I can discuss something I know and can do: a certain genre of light, pleasant fiction, which, in the interest of accuracy, I call the costume novel. The word "historical" won't do at all. I have repeatedly loaded them with history, only to have ninety-nine and ninety-nine one-hundredths of said history land on the Dial Press cutting-room floor. Which is not a complaint. That is exactly where it belongs. For, at bottom, the novelist's job is to entertain. If he aspires to instruct, or to preach, he has chosen his profession unwisely.

I believe I can write the costume novel with a fair average of success. I have made a rather serious study of the elements that go to make up a novel of wide appeal. In fact, I made this study immediately prior to writing *The Foxes of Harrow,* in order to eliminate, as far as was humanly possible, the chances of its failing.

My reasons for doing so may or may not be of interest. I had been writing all my life; my first ludicrously immature verses, mostly sonnets in rather sweet sickly imitation of Millay—with an occasional *lointain* bow in the direction of Shakespeare—were published in the little, arty magazines when I was seventeen years old. But, as I grew older, the conviction that an unpublished writer, or even one published but unread, is no writer at all began insidiously to impress itself upon me. The idea dawned that to continue to follow the route I had mapped out for myself was roughly analogous to shouting one's head off in Mammoth Cave. Rather unsatisfactory things, echoes of one's own feeble voice. I made for, and to, myself the usual excuses: I was just too intelligent, too *avant-garde* for the average mind, and so on.

But I am cursed with a rather painful sense of honesty; once past my teens, this nonsense began to have an increasingly hollow ring. University courses in English and American literature showed me one thing very surely: real talent is seldom, if ever, neglected in the world of letters—even during the lifetime of the writer. Offhand, I can think of but three exceptions: Nathaniel Hawthorne, Walt Whitman, and Herman Melville. They managed to be really *avant-garde* for their times, which, in our basically imitative profession, is no mean feat. A wise teacher pointed out to me another fact: the classics of today are very nearly always the best sellers of the past. Thackeray, Dickens, Defoe, Byron, Pope, Fielding—the list is endless—enjoyed fabulous popularity in their day. And, crossing the channel, what can one say of Balzac, Hugo, Maupassant, Dumas?

Once having been forced to admit the unpalatable truth: a writer is unread only because he fails to communicate, has not really mastered his craft, I was faced with a greater problem: how the blazes does one get published—and, more important, read? It took me years to stumble upon the solution, which I found, oddly enough, in a magazine devoted to ancient automobiles! I was thumbing through this magazine when my eye was caught by a photo of a car with no less than *eight* wheels. The caption stated, in effect, that this vehicle had failed to capture the imagination of the public, because the designer had insisted upon giving the buyers more wheels than they wanted. Other models illustrated had three wheels. They likewise failed, presumably because the automotive public found that number too few. No one, it seems, had heard of consumer research in those days.

So, neither three wheels nor eight, then. But how many wheels does the public want? The analogy was plain. One of the basic elements of the writer's temperament is a certain species of megalomania; when one thinks of it, the unmitigated gall it takes to believe steadfastly that one's mere words set down upon paper about imaginary people in imaginary situations could possibly be of interest to anyone is nothing short of stupendous. Yet we carry our delusions of grandeur to even greater lengths: we, most of us, insist upon writing what *we* want to write, and then have the naïveté to be surprised and hurt when the readers stay away from the bookstores in droves. How long would a doctor survive if he insisted upon removing the tonsils of a man with an inflamed appendix because *he* prefers tonsillectomies? Or a man who builds cars with eight wheels when four are jolly well enough?

Therefore, having collected a houseful of rejection slips for works about ill-treated factory workers, or people who suffered because of their religions or the color of their skins, I arrived at the awesome conclusion that the reader cares not a snap about such questions; that, moreover, they are none of the novelist's business. Sociologists, reformers, and ministers of the Gospel have been handling those matters rather well over the years; why not, then, let them continue? The writer is, or should be, concerned with individuals. They may be workers, Negroes, Jews, if you will; but they must be living people, with recognizably individual problems, and confronted with individual, personified opposition, not Prejudice, Bigotry, and what-have-you in capital letters. Those problems exist; but they are awfully hard to pin down in interesting fashion. The reader will believe in Tobias Skinflint, the hard hearted banker; he balks when the antagonist is "The Bank."

From there on, my primary venture into consumer research was easy. I set myself two criteria: the novels I selected for study must be those which have passed a double test: *i.e.,* they must have been successful when published, and must have continued to be successful over the years. I reread then *Tom Jones, Vanity Fair, Moll Flanders, Wuthering Heights, Jane Eyre, Joseph Andrews* among others. I read no contemporary novels, not out of prejudice against my fellows, but because I was searching for those elements of the novelist's art which have weathered the test of time.

All of these books, I already knew, met both qualifications: they were read then; they are being read, now. What I wanted to find out was why. The whys soon became obvious: they are all good, rousing tales, and fun to read. They all end—except *Wuthering Heights*—more or less happily; and their characters, carefully studied, were a revelation. The cardinal point about Tom Jones, Joseph Andrews, Becky Sharp, Moll, Heathcliff, Rochester, *et al.,* is that they are not at all like the man who lives next door. They may or may not be realistic; only their contemporaries would have been qualified to discuss that point. I suspect that they aren't. One needs only to read Terence, Plautus, or Seneca to realize how little human nature has changed in two thousand years. (If it has changed at all, which I doubt) What they are is interesting, even exciting. All these authors—Fielding, the Brontës, Defoe, Thackeray—have achieved the novelist's highest attainment: not the still life of literal representation of people and events—which would be a thumping bore—but a magistral suspension of the reader's sense of disbelief.

From them I drew certain basic rules which I have subsequently ignored only at grave peril. These rules are my own. They very probably would not work for anyone else. But, for whatever they may be worth, here they are:

The protagonist must be picaresque. In other words, he must be a charming scoundrel, preferably with a dark secret in his past. His antisocial tendencies must be motivated by specific reasons—an unfortunate childhood, injustices heaped upon himself or upon his loved ones, physical and moral sufferings which incline the reader to sympathize with his delinquency. He must be a doer, never resignedly submitting to the blows of fate; but initiating the action of the plot himself.

Curiously enough, he must be a dominant male. I think this quality appeals most of all to American women readers. For, after having had their mothers and grandmothers convert the United States into a matriarchy with their ardent femininism, and reduce the bearded patriarch that grandfather was into the pink and paunchy Casper Milquetoast of today, the average American female reader subconsciously enjoys reading about a male who can get up on his hind legs and roar. They will deny this statement, hotly. Nevertheless, it is so.

Physically, he can be of almost any type except short, bald, and bearded. These taboos, since women make up a large part of the costume novel's readers, are absolute. He should not be too good-looking, or the more sophisticated will doubt him. But exciting to look upon, he must be. And "romantic"—a curious word meaning all things to all people. From my point of view, it means that in his emotional relationships he should not be too bright—something, perhaps, that I should not state so baldly. But again and again the action of the costume novel's plot is carried forward by our hero's failure to realize that in any man's life there are literally dozens, if not hundreds, of women who will do just as well; that he won't die if he doesn't win fair Susan's dainty hand; and that very probably he will catch a most uninteresting variety of hell if he does win it. Which, come to think of it, is not unrealistic: emotional maturity is one of the rarest qualities in life.

All of the above applies also to the heroine, or, preferably heroines, since my conviction that the male of the species is incurably polygamous remains unshaken. The little dears should, of course, be a trifle less picaresque, except when, as in the case of Moll Flanders or Becky Sharp, they are the protagonists. They can, in the costume novel, approach real loveliness; for feminine readers tend to identify themselves with their fictional heroines and so can accept female beauty. And they must be even more emotionally immature, that is romantic, than the protagonist. The reader will accept the portrait of the at-first unloved, but ever so much finer, little creature's waiting for years until the opportunity presents itself to win our Jonathan; which, in life, happens about as frequently as being struck by lightning. I never cease to marvel at the reader's willingness to catch John Donne's falling star, and to attempt that impossibly intimate feat with his mandrake root. These aspects of the costume novel sometimes distress me; but, there they are.

The heroine must have an aura of sex about her. When I reach this point, I must admit that I am writing about a thing of which I am entirely unsure. I have held, at different times, quite opposite points of view about literary sex. I once believed it essential to popular success; then, later, I believed it fatal to that success. Now, I just don't know. I find writing about sex childish, boring, and distressing; but I find a too careful avoidance of the subject artificial. After all, with the exception of some individuals held back by religious scruples, most people do have a regular sex life. I am inclined to think now that the way of handling the subject is all important. If it can be done with enough delicacy, tact, indirection, implication, understatement, it can help a novel. If not, better let it alone. I have often longed for our Victorian forebears' delightfully contrived phrase: "Let us now draw the curtain of charity over the ensuing scene."

To illustrate, *Foxes of Harrow* has very little sex in it. And that little occurs behind Victorian curtains, carefully drawn. But, in my next work, a novel entitled *Ignoble Victory* (far better written, I stubbornly insist upon believing, than anything I have ever done before or since) I ran into difficulties. It was, in a way, literary. I was solemnly assured that it would lose me the public I had gained. One of my editors kept writing me pithy memos: "More sex, Frank! For goodness sake, more sex!" So I went overboard. *Ignoble Victory* was downgraded into *The Vixens,* a book I have never since been able to read. I can get as far as the point where Denise appears with her violet eyes, miraculous figure, and untamed libido. Then my stomach revolts. Perhaps I am wrong. *The Vixens* had impressive sales. I think, however, that it was bought by readers of *The Foxes,* hoping for more of the same. To them, my humblest apologies. It should have been banned, or burned.

I hotly insisted that it wasn't its overcharged sexiness that made it sell. Then the letters began to come in. They were better than 90 per cent pro-sex. Later, I made an interesting discovery: the many, many readers whose good taste must have been offended, almost surely didn't write. Because those approving letters were so alike as almost to have been written by one hand. They made me sorrowfully remember the remark of a healthy profane, if somewhat ungrammatical friend: "God help them as has to *read* about it."

So I toned sex down again. In some books, such as *A Woman Called Fancy* and *The Treasure of Pleasant Valley,* I all but eliminated it. *Fancy* sold. *Treasure* didn't. Conclusion: sex neither helps nor hurts a book; it all depends upon whether the novel, itself, is interesting. But, as I said before, even of this conclusion I am not sure. I think that, depending upon how it is handled, it may do either.

The third essential of the costume novel is a strong, exteriorized conflict, personified in a continuing, formidable antagonist or antagonists. The phrase comes from my publisher, the late George Joel. I have an unfortunate habit of underplaying the villain. In the first place, to the twentieth-century mind, wickedness is equivalent to sickness, and sickness is dull. In the second, I find it impossible to believe that two people can keep up a quarrel, however vital, for four hundred pages. But no good costume novel can move unless the conflict is there. I know I am wrong, professionally, about my point of view; but it costs me great effort to keep my boys banging away at each other. I find myself wanting to say: "Why don't you idiots shake hands, have a quiet drink together, and forget it?" But, if they do, what becomes of my novel? Now I do believe in interior conflicts: man warring with himself. I have seen them go on lifelong. But these are not the stuff of the costume novel.

Once the characters, and the supporting, minor players have been assembled, they, themselves, with some slight assisting impetus from the histories, make the plot. If they don't assume life, take the bit between their teeth, and start galloping all over the landscape, they were stillborn in the first place, and it is much better to let them lie.

The plot should be lean, economical, stripped down. Life is meandering, often pointless; but a novel is not life, but a deliberate distortion of it, solely designed to give pleasure to a reader. Therefore, hewing to the line of the plot is essential; there must be no wandering for so much as a single paragraph from the point. Anything that can be cut, should be. One superfluous word is too much. Go on with your windy flights, and friend reader puts the book down and turns on the TV set. If he hasn't it on already. The trick is to make him forget that vast, moronic eye is there.

The plot should be dramatic. The reader must be snatched out of his reclining chair and set down as a participating witness in the midst of it. Therefore nothing should be told which can be shown; nothing shown which can be implied. Suggestion is always more powerful than statement, because it assures the reader's participation by forcing his imagination to supply the details that the novelist left out. And he will supply them. Doubled. And in spades.

There must, finally, be a *theme* to the novel: our characters must rise above themselves and their origins and contribute—toward the end, in one or two brief scenes—something ennobling to life. This is delicate. If Tom Jones, having been more or less a gigolo, starts acting like a scoutmaster, the results will be pretty dreary. The reader likes to believe he is going to reform, but doesn't want to hang around to witness that distressing spectacle. For these, and many other reasons, theme is the most difficult part of the costume novel.

More than in any other type of novel, the writer of costume entertainments must be concerned with the problems of individual men and women. While these problems can turn upon such themes as religion, race, politics, and economics, it is far better that they do not. Such themes by their very nature, tend to transform the novel into a propagandist's tract basket; and few novelists have the will power to prevent them from so doing. Worse, using them, most novelists succumb to the temptation to put their own burning opinions into the mouths of their characters, thus reducing them out of life into puppets dancing on very visible strings. I cannot repeat often enough that the novelist's concern is not what interests himself, but what interests his readers. Negatively, therefore, he should avoid themes about which he has fixed opinions. He cannot do them justice. He is very likely mistaken, and attendant circumstances modify the rightness or wrongness of a thing totally. Even murder can be an entirely moral action under special circumstances of absolute necessity.

I have mentioned that in my early days, I, too, employed the themes I now avoid like the plague, in one or two so-called proletarian novels so typical of the depression epoch. Like all the young in body or in mind, I then believed that all problems can be solved; and that it was my duty to help solve them through my sterling prose. But I grew up in the late thirties, a period that went out of its way to educate a man. I rapidly arrived at the conviction I have held ever since: that many, if not most of life's problems cannot be solved at all. Build a dam on the Nile, and the starving fellaheen, better fed from the increased productivity of their newly irrigated lands, grow strong enough to produce an explosion in the birthrate, so that the next generation has half as much to eat as their fathers had before the dam.

I no longer believe that all peoples should be Christian or live under a democracy. I find the fact deplorable that an overwhelming majority of mankind, including, I am sure, very many so-called liberals, instinctively dislike people with different colored skins, oddly—to them—textured hair, and eyes aslant. But they always have. And they always will. The best we can do is to make the cost of acting upon their prejudices legally prohibitive. The prejudices themselves are immune to legislation, reason, or Christian charity.

What then, are we shouting about? Life is too short for wasted motions in writing as in all else. Besides, pragmatically, if we serve up, lightly browned, themes which run counter to the way the reader really feels, though he may be too civilized or too prudent to admit it, we are again offering him for his hard-earned money that eight-wheeled car. In proof of which, one needs but read Cozzens' masterfully crafted *By Love Possessed.* One of the reasons for its success was, I submit, that Cozzens managed to make the unfortunate American tendency toward anti-Semitism and anti-Catholicism very nearly intellectually respectable. People want their prejudices, and their beliefs, however unethical, confirmed, not attacked. To confirm them is, of course, as nearly immoral as anything is in this world. But one can hold one's tongue. And with dignity. Whining about one's lot ill becomes a man.

What, then, are the good and useful themes? Even, often, the great themes? First, I should list the unsolvable problem of evil. MacLeish has tackled it, I understand, wonderfully in *J. B.* Second, man against himself, which is, *au fond,* the root of all problems: the mature, the emotionally secure, the psychologically healthy don't need the compensatory behavior mechanisms of prejudice and hate. Third, man's relationship with God, which is but a projection of his relationship with himself, greatly idealized. Fourth, the eternal warfare of the sexes, with its fitful, biologically imposed truces. Beyond these four, I decline to proceed; because all the lesser, though still important themes, are actually matters of taste. As an afterthought, I might except the theme of man faced with death, measuring up, or failing to, to the fact that he is finite, trying to face the termination of all his hopes, beliefs, dreams with dignity and pride, or groveling abjectly in terror before the inevitability of his fate. That is a true theme, and hardly a matter of taste. But all the rest are. There is an apt saying here in Spain: *"Sobre gustos, no hay nada escrito."* ("Of tastes, there is nothing written.")

I have nibbled at the edges of all these themes. They are, admittedly, too big for my slim talent. Perhaps they are beyond any writer's skill, but they should be tried. As Faulkner says, "We shall be judged by the splendor of our failures." I have, I think, been somewhat successful with Theme Four. Like most men in their forties, I have marched, and retreated, in the ranks. With the other three, I have failed; but, I like to think, not utterly. And as far as Theme One, the problem of evil, is concerned, I have accepted failure from the outset. One always fails with that question, splendidly or not. It is not a defeat to be ashamed of; the greatest intelligences of all times have come a cropper on that one, too.

Inescapably, the costume novel belongs to what has been called escape literature. I have often wondered, with weary patience, why that term is used by critics as a dirty word. Considered coldly, what kind of fiction is not escapist? The route indicated by the novelist may differ markedly; but the destination is still the never-never land of the spirit, of imagination; and all the arrows point away from the here and now. Your writer guide may take you through the South Side of Chicago, down Los Angeles' Skid Row, rub your refined nostrils in the raw odors of realism; but you know, and he knows, that you don't read his opus if you live on the South Side, Skid Row, or the Bowery—or even if you happen to be a *clochard* sleeping in the cold and wet under one of the bridges of the Seine.

If he is honest, as he so seldom is, the novelist will admit that at best he is aiming for a carefully contrived, hypnotic suspension of his reader's sense of disbelief—not ever for a real slice of life. Because, in life, people think of the proper response two hours, or two days, too late; things go wrong, not upon the respectable scale of tragedy, but on the slow, bumbling, painfully embarrassing, minuscule dimensions of inept, amateur farce. In life, conversation is an endless series of *non sequiturs,* of windy nonsense, or of just plain dull nonsense. And no realist would ever dare pinpoint on paper the most realistic of all life's attributes: the thundering, crashing boredom of the life of the average man.

The point of all this is, I suppose, that novels written with the deliberate intention to amuse and entertain have—or should have—a very real place in contemporary literature. It seems to me that people have the right to escape occasionally and temporarily from life's sprawling messiness, satisfy their hunger for neat patterns, retreat into a dreamlife where boy gets girl and it all comes out right in the end always. They need such escapes to help them endure the shapelessness of modern existence. It is only when they try to escape permanently that the trip out to Kansas and Karl Menninger's becomes indicated. I honestly believe that thumbing through an occasional detective yarn, science-fiction tale, or costume novel, is rather better preventive therapy than tranquilizers, for instance.

It has been some time since I checked, but I don't think our constitutional right to the pursuit of happiness has been repealed.

CHAPTER 12

Writers and Their Editors

Notes on an Uneasy Marriage

JOHN FISCHER

Several years ago, when my main job was editing books, I began to wonder whether it might be possible to introduce at least a trace of scientific method into a wildly unscientific business.

Every day authors or their agents would come in to get money to finance the writing of a book. Usually they would have a couple of chapters finished and an outline of the rest. Sometimes they had nothing but an idea, in their heads or scribbled on the back of an old envelope. (One agent, whose effrontery I have always admired, didn't even have that. She said she represented a radio commentator, and she suggested that if a publisher would put up $10,000 so that he could lie on a Florida beach and think for a few weeks, he might bring back an outline for a possible book.)

On such tenuous security, publishers frequently advance sums ranging from $500 to several thousand dollars—to be repaid out of the author's royalty, if and when he delivers a manuscript which can be published and sold to a far-from-eager public. The decision is made almost entirely on the basis of sheer hunch—or what publishers prefer to describe, wistfully, as "editorial judgment." The editor takes a look at whatever the author has down on paper; checks the sales and reviews of his previous books, if any; finds out what he can about any recent books on a similar theme; wonders whether the buying public will have any interest in the subject when the book is published, maybe two years later; makes a personal estimate of the writer's talent, responsibility, and character—and then takes a deep breath and decides how much of the firm's money to gamble. (Even when there is no advance to the author, publishing a book requires an investment of at least $5,000.)

If an editor guesses wrong too often, he and his firm will be out of business. Even the best make so many bad guesses that every publishing house has to write off thousands of dollars in unearned advances each year. And the mistake of being overcautious can be equally serious; I remember with shame at least five authors whose demands I turned down as exorbitant, and who are now bringing in fat, green wads of money for rival firms.

So—like many another naïve young editor—I started to look for some clue which might help me to calculate on a less haphazard basis whether any given author would be likely to earn enough to repay the money he asked for. I made a careful study of the performance records of some two hundred writers, looking for common characteristics which would distinguish the good risks from the bad.

Two showed up. Nearly all the successful writers had them, while the failures did not. They were:

1. An abnormal supply of simple animal energy.
2. An overcharged ego.

This discovery proved less than revolutionary, because there is another essential ingredient—talent—which I never did learn to spot with any certainty until the writer had demonstrated it on paper, and not always then. Plenty of would-be authors are endowed with Napoleonic ego and the energy of a terrier pup, but still can't write a lick. Yet it also seems to be generally true that the most luminous talent won't get very far when the other two qualities are missing.

As a scientific finding, this may not amount to much, but for an editor it does have its uses. In addition to cutting down his bad debt figures, it can help him in developing a working partnership with his authors. For, once they have entered into their curious alliance, the editor's main jobs are then: (a) to keep his writer churning out manuscripts and (b) to nourish, protect, and shepherd that all-important ego.

The first chore is relatively straightforward. If the writer possesses that overflowing vitality which has characterized such diverse specimens as Tolstoi, Edgar Wallace, Tom Wolfe, and Dickens, he will write as naturally as a fire burns. The publisher will have to sell enough books to stoke the auctorial flames with their necessary fuel: money. On occasion he may also need to offer advice about markets, syntax, and organization of subject matter, and to prune back the luxuriant prose which unbridled energy so often produces. But if the sheer physical drive isn't there, the case is hopeless. Writing is a punishing trade, and the feeble soon drop it.

But there is nothing simple about the editor's second duty. Ego-nursing will take a different form with every author—but, like baby-raising, it always ought to begin with affection and respect. If an editor doesn't like authors enough to put up with their tantrums and change their emotional diapers, he is in the wrong business.

And he must understand that if a writer's ego ever wilts, he is ruined. It is the only thing that can sustain him through those lonely months while he is trying to piece together a book out of one recalcitrant word after another. Every morning he has to persuade himself, all over again, that putting marks on paper is the most important thing in the world . . . that he has something to say which thousands of people not only will listen to, but pay for . . . that it has not been said already (or anyhow not so well) by his innumerable competitors, from Homer to O'Hara . . . and therefore that his personal statement of Eternal Truth has to be recorded at all costs, even if his children starve and his neglected wife takes up canasta.

Only an ego-maniac can believe these things, for they defy all the evidence. Any rational man could see that far too many books already are being published . . . that only a small fraction of them can possibly be reviewed . . . that even these usually will encounter an invincible indifference . . . that most books are nearly as perishable as fresh vegetables, and soon doomed to be pushed off the store shelves by a fresh crop . . . that the odds therefore are overwhelmingly against any given writer making a ripple on the public consciousness. Or even making a living. For reasons noted in some of these articles the average novelist can rarely hope to earn as much per year as the linotypist who sets his books in type.

Yet if his ego is sturdy enough, an author can ignore these facts and turn again to his typewriter, confident that he is not like other men, and that *his* book will beat the odds. And sometimes he is right.

That is why one veteran editor, William Sloane, once described his work as a cross between playing the horses and practicing medicine without a license. It is a kind of psychotherapy, a process of reassuring the writer constantly that his genius is unique, that the last chapter was a gem, and that the world breathlessly awaits his message.

Nor is this hypocrisy. It is true that an editor has to view the literary facts of life more realistically than a writer dares to, and that sometimes he has to administer flattery in doses that would gag an opera star. But, allowing for this therapeutic hyperbole, the editor believes what he says. He thinks his boy has what it takes, and he is backing this conviction with a big piece of the firm's money.

Phony enthusiasm, in fact, just doesn't work. The writer will soon spot it, and so will the salesmen who eventually will have to try to persuade somebody to read the finished book. So a capacity for real (and soundly-based) enthusiasm is perhaps the greatest asset an editor can have. For example, the way in which Alfred Knopf's unsquelchable enthusiasm for Joseph Conrad finally created an American market for his works is still a legend of the trade.

Yet the editor cannot afford to let his author's ego get completely out of hand. He has to nurture and restrain it, both at once—a task always delicate, and sometimes impossible. He has to sort out the writer's delusions—tolerating and even encouraging those which are useful, while at the same time trying to curb those which are destructive.

The editor of a publishing house which specializes in light fiction once told me that he had worked for years with a highly successful woman novelist. Rarely in all that time did she ever talk about anything except her dominant obsession: the shameful way in which she was neglected and abused by her husbands, children, reviewers, booksellers, publishers, and public. Actually, he said, she was a pampered old dragon who got her own way in nearly everything and tyrannized the lives of everybody within reach. But her illusion was indispensable for her work. All her novels dealt with the same theme—the piteous fate of woman in an unfeeling world—and since this appealed to the streak of self-pity in millions of female readers, her books sold very well indeed. If she had ever been forced to confront the truth, she probably could never have written another line.

Again, I was puzzled for a long time by the conviction of most unsuccessful writers that no publisher will read a manuscript unless it is thrust into his unwilling hands by a friend, a wealthy aunt, or the banker who holds the mortgage on the printing press. Repeatedly I tried to explain that reading manuscripts is a publisher's business, that he gives them careful attention, whether they are delivered by the postman, an agent,* or his own mother; that, in fact, publishers are constantly on the prowl for new talent. Hardly anybody was convinced.

At last it dawned upon me that not-yet-successful writers need this myth, and that it is both useless and cruel to try to dispel it.

---

* Nearly a hundred literary agencies are now operating in New York. Perhaps a dozen of these have earned the full confidence of most publishing houses, because they understand the problems of both authors and editors and never submit anything which is not a real possibility for a particular publisher's list. Consequently, manuscripts from them often get prompter attention: but no reputable firm ever declines a manuscript, from any source, without at least one responsible reading.

Suppose you have labored for two years over The Great American Novel, investing in it all the passion and talent at your command. Then it is rejected in quick succession by eleven publishers. There can be two possible explanations:

1. Nobody ever read it—or at best it was skimmed by some callow, coke-drinking junior reader, who couldn't recognize genius if it kicked him in the teeth.
2. The novel is no good.*

Which would you believe? Which would you *have* to believe, if you planned to embark on another novel?

This necessity for maintaining an unshakable faith in his own talent sometimes leads an author into fantasies which are less benign. It then becomes the editor's responsibility to disillusion him. However tactful the editor may be, the process is always painful; and it is this which so often makes their relationship a tense and unstable one.

For instance, when the sale of a book is disappointing, the author always knows who's to blame. If it had been advertised properly—with billboards, skywriting, and TV commercials—if only the publisher had seen to it that the *New York Times* reviewed this work, instead of wasting its space on Faulkner and Hemingway—then surely the public would have discovered it, in carload lots.

At this juncture the editor may try to explain that the firm already has spent far more on advertising than the book could hope to earn . . . that book reviewers can neither be pressured nor cajoled, and that any publisher who tries will soon regret it . . . that the public seems to be tiring of sensitive novels about the torments of adolescence . . . that a sale of 3,182 copies of a first novel really is pretty good . . . and that maybe we will all have better luck with the next

---

*A third possibility is that eleven experienced editors read it—and all of them guessed wrong. This has happened, with the result that a twelfth publisher profited from their mistakes; but such cases are extremely rare.

one, especially if the narrative pace is a little faster. These home truths are no comfort to the author.* Quite possibly they will merely encourage him to look for another publisher.

The same thing may happen when the editor offers advice on a manuscript. It may be his plain duty to point out that the heroine sounds like a fifth carbon of Scarlett O'Hara, and that a thirty thousand word description of Terre Haute in 1890 might well be cut out of the opening chapter. The writer may recognize these hints as sound and accept them gratefully. Or—you never can tell—he may regard them as a vote of no-confidence and a Philistine assault upon the integrity of his work.

For this reason, it is never wise to show a reader's report to an author. Such reports are probably the best literary criticism being written anywhere. They often sum up the strengths, weaknesses, sales potential, and literary stature of a manuscript with remarkable precision. The *New Yorker* recently observed, in a memorial note about the late Wolcott Gibbs, that if his written editorial opinions "could be released to the world (as they most assuredly can't be), they would make probably a funnier and sounder critique of creative writing in the late twenties and early thirties than has ever been assembled." But such reports customarily are written with a succinct, pitiless candor which might easily wound an author to his very gizzard. Consequently a prudent editor keeps the original in a locked file, and transmits the gist of it to the author in gentler (not to say muffled) terms.

Another thing which some writers find hard to tolerate is the idea that an editor is not a private possession, like a one-man dog. This type (fortunately not very common) wants full-time, undivided attention, not only to his literary affairs, but also to his plane

---

*Nothing is—short of astronomical sales and undiluted acclaim. And nobody is immune to the pangs of authorship. Between stints of editing, I once wrote a couple of books myself. To my astonishment, I found that I developed all the standard symptoms, although I knew perfectly well that my expectations were silly and my demands unreasonable.

reservations, theater tickets, and romantic tangles. Any reminder that the editor now and then has to deal with the problems of other authors is likely to touch off a spasm of jealous anger, accompanied in extreme cases by accusations of neglect and disloyalty. This syndrome (at least in my experience) occurs most frequently among women; perhaps it has something to do with their innate prejudice against polygamy.

But the author's ego is not the only potential source of friction. Editors also have egos which can cause trouble, and with far less justification.

The main danger here is that the editor may try, consciously or unconsciously, to impose his own conceptions on the writer. This is most apt to happen if the editor is himself a frustrated author; he may then, usually without realizing it, attempt to influence a novelist to produce the epic *he* had wanted to create. The upshot almost surely will be a disaster for everybody.

Or an editor may grow dogmatic. If he ever begins to think that he knows exactly how every kind of book ought to be written, and that he can guess infallibly what the public wants, then he is coming down with that special form of *hubris* which is the occupational disease of his profession. It will make him miss both the truly original work of art and the good commercial item which—according to conventional rules—should be unsalable.

I hate to remember the time when James R. Newman first told me his scheme for a history of mathematics. We were working together on a wartime intelligence assignment which had taken us to London, and one evening while we were drinking beer in his room at the Athenaeum Court Hotel he outlined his project. He wanted to gather all the basic documents of mathematical thought and arrange them into an anthology which would trace the development of the science in the words of the masters themselves. It would be a big book, perhaps 500 pages. What did I think of it?

I told him it was impossible. Nobody would buy it; its subject was too specialized—in fact to most people (including me) downright repellent—and it would be far too costly to manufacture. Why didn't he turn his energies to something practical, such as a book on chess—a subject on which he was equally expert? Jim said he was bored with chess.

A week or so later he said he had revised his plan. He now thought the book should be two volumes, a really comprehensive work. Did that make it sound more promising? I said no, it sounded worse. The next night I flew to North Africa.

We didn't meet again until the war was over. Jim then told me that he had been plugging away at his anthology, in spite of my advice; that it had grown to four volumes; and that Simon & Schuster was going to publish it. I was dumbfounded: S & S, always known as a real shrewd outfit, must have lost their minds.

The rest is almost too humiliating for me to repeat. As everybody in the trade now knows, Newman's *The World of Mathematics* became a phenomenon of publishing. Priced at an impossible $25, it sold more than 120,000 sets—in addition to distribution by two book clubs—and is still selling a steady three thousand copies a year. It also shattered my confidence in my publishing judgment, probably for good.

But all this may be giving a wrong impression. In spite of such calamities, the editing of books is one of the more cheerful trades. It has all the excitement of gambling. (Before I got into it, I used to play poker quite a lot, though badly; afterwards, I found I got enough action in the daytime.) Exasperating as they sometimes are, writers are seldom dull, and no two are alike; so the business has none of the monotony which must afflict a manufacturer of, say, canned milk. But the biggest psychic income is the editor's feeling that he often helps to bring to birth a talent or an idea. He can, in his better moments, think of himself as a midwife to the culture of his time—a part of the process by which civilization is created, preserved, and handed on from one generation to another.

In his bad moments, though, an editor may feel that his profession is almost as painful as an undertaker's. The really depressing part has nothing to do with the wrong guesses or the trying habits of authors. It is just the constant necessity of saying: "No."

For he must spend most of his working hours in being mean to people. Every manuscript accepted must be winnowed out of a stack of hundreds which are hopeless. Many of those rejected can be sent back with a form letter, but, for a variety of reasons, a surprising number require an explanation from the editor. Either by mail or face-to-face, he must tell the author that his child was stillborn, that all his labor, ambition, and emotional investment have come to nothing.

This always hurts; or should hurt. I have a notion that any editor has only so many "No's" in his system. Some have a lot, others only a few. When they are all used up, he can't stand being mean any longer, and he dies. Or—what amounts to the same thing—he gets so calloused that he can say "No" without a twinge; when that happens he is dead and doesn't know it.

CHAPTER 13

Letter to a Young Man About to Enter Publishing

ANONYMOUS

You want to go into publishing because you love good books and would like to help produce them. Fine. You are entering an extremely intricate business whose ways will take you years to learn. I can only outline for you some of our present confusion.

Perhaps the first thing you should know about is the curious attitude of the American reader. There are plenty of experts around who will prove to you that he doesn't like to spend much money on good books; that he would rather have bad books when he buys at all; that he prefers sporting equipment, drive-in movies, and television to either. For instance, Mr. Edward Weeks in the *Atlantic Monthly:*

> If I had to guess I should say that there are about one million discriminating readers in this country today and what disturbs me as an editor is that this number has not increased with the population; it has not increased appreciably since 1920. What has increased is the public appetite for comic books, for murder mysteries, for sex, for sadism.

If you want some statistics, here are some from that excellent source, the London *Economist:*

Even before television, Americans had not acquired the habit of reading good books. It has been estimated that since 1946, spending on books and maps has declined from 15 to only 10 per cent of total outlays on recreation.

If you are not convinced, here is an even blacker view. It comes from Mr. John Unterecker, an English instructor at Columbia who recently examined the publishing business for John Wain's *Literary Annual:*

> The average American spends almost precisely the same amount of money on household stationery as he does on books. In 1956, the average man spent five times as much on radio, television, musical instruments, and records as he did on books and more than twice as much on "non-durable toys." . . .
>
> The American by and large prefers to books his daily newspaper which he reads quite carefully, picture magazines such as *Life* and *Look* which can reach respectively an adult audience of 32,100,000 and 27,000,000, and the *Reader's Digest* which is read each month by 34,950,000 Americans over ten years of age.
>
> The typical American regards reading as work and prefers in his free hours to be distracted by entertainments which range from hell-fire revival meetings through professional sports contests, to drive-in motion pictures, and for winter nights, television and radio. . . .

If typical Americans regard reading as work, the publishers have at least some idea of the untypical who regard it as a pleasure. As Mr. Dan Lacy of the American Book Publishers Council recently put it:

> The basic nature of the trade-book audience is well known; it is largely urban; somewhat more women than men buy books; a dominant proportion of the reading public is in the higher professional and economic brackets; *perhaps about 2 per cent of the people account for a vital percentage of trade-book purchases.*

Who is to blame? Mr. Unterecker thinks, and not unreasonably, that some of the fault lies with the public schools who make literature "dull, difficult, and painful—dull, because it is made available only if it is harmless or has been rendered harmless by unmerciful bowdlerizing; difficult and painful because the student reads so little that he never really learns to read at all." In four years of English, he points out, the normal high-school student is required to read no more than a dozen books; and these are too seldom taught in a way that will outmatch the appeal of the omnipresent comic books or the Mickey Spillane mysteries that pass around the locker-rooms.

It would seem, wouldn't it, that you are headed for the wrong business? Perhaps you'd best go over to the personnel department at CBS. In fact, however, the publishing business has not been quite so bad as Mr. Unterecker might lead you to think. The men who run the publishing companies tend to complain about their troubles together but you may well find them doing it at their large country houses in the hills of Westchester or while touring rather grandly through the Italian hill towns.

It is only fair to say, however, that you can't expect such opulence yourself for a long while, if at all. As a matter of fact, you'll often find that a good deal of it was acquired when taxes were low and that somewhere in the background lies an inheritance or a family business more profitable than publishing. And frankly, it wouldn't hurt a bit if you had something of the sort in your own background. The American publishing industry, as the *Economist* recently commented, "still treats editorial positions rather like lieutenancies in an eighteenth-century army."

One reason it can is that there seem to be plenty of bright young men like yourself with MA's in English literature—or, simply, friends and relatives in publishing houses—who are willing to start work at about eighty dollars a week. I know of a young editor at a respected and profitable old house who put in an intensive first year during which he read hundreds of manuscripts, lured several promising young author friends to his publisher's list, and supervised the publication of books in which his bosses had invested hundreds of thousands of dollars. Finally he was able to report to his wife that he'd been given a raise—to $90.50 a week.*

It is not surprising that young editors, reading surveys like Mr. Unterecker's, scraping along on less income than the waiters who serve up their expense-account lunches, brood and wonder if publishers are supposed to turn a profit at all. At first glance it seems impossible. The fact is, and it is one of the least understood facts of the trade, that the average hard cover book published in this country doesn't sell enough copies to repay the publisher's investment in it. In its recent survey of the American book industry, the London *Economist* noted that "The publisher who sells three to four thousand copies of a book is fortunate if he recovers his out-of-pocket costs even on a relatively expensive book. . . . And the chart of a publisher's sales is likely to show a plateau at or below the 4,000 mark." Furthermore the publisher's production costs—for paper, printing, and overhead—have doubled since 1940, but the prices of books have risen less than 70 per cent.

What must the publisher do to survive? He has, you'll find, several strategies which, if shrewdly followed, can make publishing profitable.

(1) He tries to find and promote books which will leap beyond the average and have large sales. If he succeeds it can make an enormous difference to his company: St. Martin's Press, one of the smaller New York houses, was able nearly to triple its income the

---

*Like so many of the young men who go into publishing he had thought of editing as mostly a matter of fiction. He found, as do most editors, that much of his work involved finding, encouraging, and editing books of political reportage, biography, history, popular psychology, and other kinds of non-fiction. In ten years, incidentally, he can expect to make $7,500 to $10,000. The top editors in the business make more than $20,000 a year.

year it published a best seller called *Anatomy of a Murder.* But forecasting the public appeal of a book is a fearfully tricky thing to do, especially if it is a more or less serious book for the general reader by an author not widely known. It was perhaps not difficult for the publishers to predict that *'Twixt Twelve and Twenty,* the "helpful talks to teenagers" by Mr. Pat Boone, would be a national best seller. But most publishers were surprised by the extraordinary sales of *Lolita* and *Dr. Zhivago;* and, just recently, Jacques Barzun's *House of Intellect,* published in a modest first printing, became an immediate best seller. (Publishers, you'll find, are more often surprised than they let on.)

Look at some of the explanations reported to *Publishers' Weekly* this year for good book sales: Among the "greatest single helps" in selling their books, publishers mentioned ads and reviews in the *New York Times;* "publicity on such TV shows as 'Today'"; "merchandising kits" and "display racks" and circulars mailed directly to readers. One publisher said: "The best sales aid continues to be an intelligent reviewer in a strong medium; however there are fewer and fewer intelligent reviews in strong and weak media." All of these publishers could well have been right, and yet each of the "helps" has often failed dismally, sometimes at great cost. Word-of-mouth recommendations by readers who have read the books undoubtedly play a crucial role and publishers continually puzzle over how they can get people to talk about their books.

But the fact is that the publishers know far too little about American readers and they have much less direct contact with them than they should. Other industries, richer and more concentrated, have worked out elaborate techniques (a) for sampling the public's desires, (b) for effective advertising in many media, and (c) for merchandising in stores. The hard-cover publishing industry is weak in all three departments, especially the last. It is split up among hundreds of competing publishers who must operate at a low margin and have small budgets for advertising and research;* it must distribute chiefly through a few thousand widely scattered and frequently inefficient bookstores which serve far too few people.

Depressingly enough, there were more bookstores operating in the U.S. in the late nineteenth century than there are today, although the population has more than doubled. A publisher's *secret* estimate of the number of bookstores which stock a strong representation of the lists of the major publishers and do a reasonable job of selling might go as high as 300; probably it will be nearer 100, including the comparatively well-run chains of stores owned by Doubleday and Brentano. Of course publishers sympathize with the genteel book-lovers who set up small stores with inadequate capital in hopeless locations. But too often the whole situation results in a costly over-production of books people don't see, know about, or want to buy. Overproduction is one of the publisher's nightmares; another is the number of readers who walk the streets and might buy all kinds of books if only they passed a good bookstore; but they don't.

In the last few years some of the trade publishers have been try-ing both to teach the retail trade to sell effectively and also to get in closer touch with the public itself by mailing circulars listing

---

* It is not that the publishers are niggardly; for each dollar of sales, they spend twenty times as much on advertising as the auto industry. Their problem is that, unlike the auto and other industries, they must advertise as many as 80 new and quite different products a year. The individual budgets are so low that advertising on television and radio, for instance, has seldom been possible, although in the last year a few big publishers have been planning to advertise such potential best sellers as encyclopedias and cookbooks on radio and televi-sion. Recently it has become apparent that a careful plug for a likely book on a popular television program can make all the difference. After Mr. Alexander King appeared on the Jack Paar show, the sales of his book called *Mine Enemy Grows Older* jumped from 15,000 to 100,000. Now a new publishing company largely composed of television celebrities has been formed and the partners— Groucho Marx and Art Linkletter among them—claim an audience of 50 mil-lion a week. Some publishers are watching its progress with considerable alarm.

books to potential readers. These and other rather complex efforts by publishers to be businesslike seem mildly promising—although the trade has yet to come to grips with the shortage of good outlets. My point is: if you can't work up interest in these questions, you'd better stay away from publishing. If you don't learn a good deal about the problems of those who must design, advertise, and sell the books, everybody suffers, *especially* the author.*

(2) Whatever his luck in bookstores, the publisher can still hope to sell his books to one of the large book clubs, sharing the royalties equally with the author. (The clubs generally rent the original plates and print their own editions.) Over five million people are obliged by their club membership to buy several books through the mail each year. In 1958 they bought 64.8 million books—more than twice the 28.2 million adult books sold in bookstores and by direct mail. Without their proceeds from book clubs—and also from sale of reprint rights which I'll discuss later—most publishers of general books could not survive.

By far the largest of the clubs is the Reader's Digest Condensed Book Club which has some *two and a half million* members and has been known to guarantee as much as $100,000 in royalties against future sales of a condensed book (which appears with several others in a one-volume edition). The Book-of-the-Month Club (with nearly 500,000 members) and the Literary Guild (about 600,000 members) can each regularly guarantee $20,000 to $40,000 against expected sales—no small sum in the publishing business. After these "Big Three," the dozens of book clubs decline in size and potential sales; nevertheless, publishers of highbrow books are very grateful for selection by the small Reader's Subscription, which can sell three or four thousand copies of a book and retrieve its costs.

---

* Some authors may indeed be grateful for your ability to make sensible suggestions about their books, and help shape them, and this will be a crucial part of your work. But whether they need such help or not, all authors will depend on you to represent their books to the publishing world and the readers in the way that will find them the widest market and make the most money.

The *Economist* estimates that, in general, "the quality of the book-club selection sticks dismally close to the lowest common denominator." Certainly this charge does not apply to a number of the smaller clubs like the Reader's Subscription, the Mid-Century Book Society, and the History Book Club, or to the more fortunate choices of the Book-of-the-Month Club; but most editors would agree privately that it is true for too many selections of the big clubs. These have brought much money to the publishers but they have *not* made up for the shortage of good bookstores; instead they have, in general, circulated a very limited selection of mediocre books to very large numbers of people.

(3) One of the best—and least compromising—publishing strategies is to develop a profitable backlist of books which will keep selling from year to year. As the *Economist* puts it:

> Every publisher cherishes his staples; his Bibles, his dictionaries, his cookery books. Between 12,000 and 13,000 books are brought out each year but the annual catalogue of books in print has almost ten times as many listings . . . the backlist accounts for half the annual business of the industry and it provides some publishers with as much as three-quarters of their business.

There is no telling what kind of book may keep selling over the years: medieval histories and apparently obscure novels may do far better than books which were best sellers in their day. Fresh from the university, you should be aware of two especially important staples: textbooks and juvenile books. The publishing industry knows its demography; it has delighted in putting out millions of textbooks for the large numbers of children born during the war and postwar years, some of whom are now entering college. And contrary to all predictions, the dreary fantasy of television seems to have driven many small children back to books instead of away from them forever. The juvenile book business is thriving* (a classic like Button's

---

* In 1958, 32.8 million juvenile books costing more than a dollar were sold—as compared with 16.8 million in 1952.

The World of Pooh sold some 200,000 copies last year) and, although they may not advertise the fact, several of the most distinguished New York publishers depend heavily on juveniles for their profits. It is even conceivable—or so the publishers pray—that the children will survive both puberty and their high-school education and go on reading when they grow up.

I'll say no more about these traditional ways of turning a publishing dollar—or about the other fundamentals of the business I've not mentioned: movie and television rights (which are *not* very valuable), libraries, agents, mysteries, mail order, and remainder houses, to name a few. Each involves a complicated commercial world in which you'll probably have to find your way, and I wish you luck. Instead, I'd ask you to consider a fourth strategy publishers use to make money, which, I suggest, is one of the most important for you to think about—the Paperback Phenomenon.

In 1958, 258 million paperback books for adults were sold as compared with 28.2 million hard-cover adult "trade books"—i.e., books of general interest sold in bookstores (as distinguished from texts, technical works, etc.). Most of the paperbacks were reprints from hard-cover books and the royalties, split equally between the original publisher and the author, were an important source of income to both. As the decline in the sales of hard-cover novels over the last ten years makes clear, the public now prefers its fiction in paperbacks; when considering a work of fiction by an unknown author, the publisher must usually reckon on losing money if he cannot arrange a reprint—or a book-club—sale. But, beyond that, the enormous predominance of paperback over hard-cover sales has been forcing hard-cover publishers to reconsider many of their old assumptions: How important *are* hard covers on books?

Certainly many publishers and writers on American culture have scarcely known what to make of the Paperback Phenomenon. Mr. Weeks, for instance, acknowledges that the general level of paperbacks has improved since the days when the racks were crowded with "lurid, large-bosomed beauties" but it seems to him "regrettable after one hundred years of public education that we

have produced such a demand for the lowest common denominator of emotionalism." On the other hand, Mr. Peter Drucker, the
well-known business consultant and expert on the American future,
recently said of paperbacks that there had been a "great shift in their
public market and content: history, foreign affairs, art, and religion
are rapidly becoming staples."

If Mr. Drucker and Mr. Weeks seem to disagree, don't let it
bother you; it is just the sort of dispute about worthiness that one
finds in the publishing business. Neither of these busy men, I suspect, has actually counted down the list of more than 6,000 paperbacks and ticked off the good, innocuous, and bad, and neither have
I. Nor, incidentally, has our old friend Mr. Unterecker, but he does
have something to say about the Paperback Phenomenon which you
should consider carefully:

> America now has 1,200 bookstores selling [a representative
> selection of] hard-cover books. But in the last twenty years paper-
> back booksellers have increased in number from several dozen
> to, early in 1958, just under 100,000. These 100,000 outlets—
> newsstands, soda fountains, department stores, bus and railroad
> terminals—make it possible for the publishers to print immense edi-
> tions. Not all these editions are of good books (7,277,000 copies of
> Grace Metalious's sex-larded *Peyton Place* are now in print) but
> many of the paperbacks are excellent.
>
> And more important, good, bad, and indifferent, the soft-cover
> books are gradually swinging the non-reading American into the
> habit of reading. Because he feels, I think for the first time, that the
> book is somehow not sacred. Literature, that terrible and dull thing
> which he had been forced in high school to read far too slowly and
> which he had been made to respect as something a little out of his
> reach, becomes, on a drugstore display rack, almost as attractive in its
> garish, enticing cover as *Life, Look,* or *Reader's Digest.* And because it
> costs very little more than those publications it becomes . . . some-
> thing that can be used and thrown away. If he doesn't respect litera-
> ture, he often discovers—to his surprise—that he likes it.
>
> Books consequently which no one in his right mind would have
> considered publishing in editions of over 3,000 copies in hard
> covers suddenly, as paperbacks, find a [large] audience.

It is this new audience for books and its developing reading habits, therefore, which seem to me ultimately responsible for some of the growing trends in American writing and publishing. No writer or publisher can now ignore this audience and everybody is feeling out rather carefully its interests.

Mr. Unterecker is rather more optimistic this time and I think he is right to be, although, as you note, he does not go into the fascinating (if not frightening) question of how well many of these books, especially the "excellent" ones are read. And unfortunately he does not go on and discuss the significant differences between Cheap and Quality Paperbacks:

Cheap paperbacks sold from those ubiquitous wire display racks, are published mainly by some half-dozen large, independent reprint houses (New American Library, Bantam, Pocket, Fawcett, Dell, etc.). The average first printing of the books is about 150,000–175,000 copies, and the royalty on a 25-cent book will start at a penny and mount along with sales. Wartime editions for servicemen helped to establish the format and create the public appeal for these books; until the early fifties, nine out of ten were fiction, and although some excellent titles got into print the business relied on a hard core of Westerns, mysteries, and sexy thrillers. Since then a clean-up movement has taken place and although the hard core is still there, some of the paperback publishers have found that the classics, modern psychology, anthropology, reprints of good novels, and innocuous light books can at least compete profitably with the tortured blondes. But if they have been converted to the classics and to the salability of Freud, Jane Austen, Ruth Benedict, and Salinger, they are still slow to put out recent books, especially non-fiction. For the present, at least, sales of cheap paperbacks seem to have reached a plateau of about 250 million a year.

Quality paperbacks are an altogether different story. They were introduced in America as recently as 1953 by a young man at Doubleday and Company, the largest hardbound publisher of all. Incorporating some of the features of the English "Penguins," he issued a line of firmly bound, nicely covered, paperbacked reprints called Anchor Books which were published for about a dollar in printings of about 20,000 at a royalty of 6 to 7½ per cent, and were supposed to appeal to college students and their teachers, in particular, and to eggheads in general. Edmund Wilson's *To the Finland Station,* David Riesman's *The Lonely Crowd,* and A. E. Taylor's *Socrates* were some of the first titles, and the trend has been for the books to be more specialized and abstruse, rather than less.

Doubleday was able to draw on its own large stock of titles for some of the Anchor Books, but for others they bought the rights from competing publishers. The publishing trade soon observed that the books were selling out in the college bookstores. Within two years a half-dozen New York publishers had entered the field with Anchor-like editions of their own and today there are literally dozens of quality paperback imprints which have issued some 2,000 titles; last year their sales reached some eight million copies—far less than the 28.2 million hardcover trade books sold to adults but impressive considering that six years ago none were sold at all, and that demand is steadily increasing.

The quality paperback boom has proved much more durable than many publishers had thought—some of the original skeptics have now introduced lines of their own. At small colleges the books have in effect made possible the sale of general books where only textbooks were once sold, while at Harvard the average student is buying twenty paperbacks a year. Many young people seem to have become impatient with hard-cover books; at Columbia the bookstore clerks found that the paperbound edition of a book of scientific philosophy was outselling the hardbound edition four to one, *at the same price.* Increasingly the books are moving off campuses into big-city outlets and even into some of the magazine stands that carry cheap paperbacks. The publishers are aware that the current college generation is becoming used to quality paperbacks. Nevertheless they tend to worry. The field is crowded: they remember that after the war the cheap paperback field included imprints such as Eagle Books, Pony Books, and Bart House which are long extinct. And they wonder how many highbrow books of history, art, philosophy, science, religion, etc., are left which will be suitable for wide distribution. No doubt it is admirable that Rudolph Carnap's difficult *Meaning and Necessity* (Phoenix) and Maud Bodkin's *Archetypal Patterns in Poetry* (Vintage) are now available to the student at low prices; but what, the publishers are wondering, lies beyond Carnap and Bodkin? How will it all end?

The most striking suggestion of how it might all end came last spring in a speech delivered to a group of publishers by Arthur A. Cohen, the founder and president of Meridian Books, a company which publishes mainly quality paperbacks, over 140 of them, including Jung, E. M. Forster, Baudelaire, Robert M. Hutchins, and Mary McCarthy.

"The thesis to which I will address myself," Cohen began, "is that paperbound publishing seems destined to obliterate cloth trade publishing as we presently know it."

In saying this to the hard-cover publishers, Cohen was somewhat in the position of a Jacobin announcing his program on the steps of Versailles; the argument he made in this speech and in subsequent memos is too long to quote to you in full but it deserves your attention.

The great trouble with the quality paperbacks, Cohen said, is that the publishers were seduced by the success of the original Anchor Books formula and assumed there must be some necessary connection between scholarly books of profound—not to say ponderous—significance and the quality paperback binding. In recent years the formula has become harder and harder to follow: "The mediocre book is now made to masquerade as definitive; it has become increasingly common for a minor work by a major author to be advertised in reverse—the name large and the title small."

And for Cohen this has been a great mistake. Far from being limited to the original highbrow formula, he thinks that the quality paperback format presents an opportunity to publish many kinds of books, at low prices, for very diverse audiences. The potential buyers of new novels, biographies, and other popular books, have, he points out, just as much difficulty buying hardcover books on their salaries as do the students, teachers, artists, and intellectuals who have bought so many scholarly and "difficult" quality paperbacks.

The quality paperbacks, Cohen insists, are not tied to subject matter. The important things about them are these: Their production is simpler and cheaper; they have more outlets; the accounting, processing, shipping, merchandising involved in their publication all lend themselves to money saving mechanization; and the capital and time saved allowed for the development of a "more imaginative editorial program."

Certainly a number of publishers are now edging away from the original Anchor formula: Viking's Compass Books and Grosset's Universal Library are reprinting some modern novels and popular books. Macmillan is launching a poet's series; Anchor and Harper's Torchbooks are introducing extensive programs of publishing in the sciences; Grove's Evergreen—which has already published many excellent works of modern fiction in paperbacks—will do a series on contemporary art; Cohen's firm will soon issue "Meridian Fiction"—"reprints directed at those who think there is something between Spillane and Lermontov"—as well as a history text series and a paperback magazine edited by Saul Bellow.

But the question still remains whether *new* books of general interest can be published originally in paperbacks, Since the difference between the cost of producing a quality paperback book and a hard-cover book is small, it is often necessary to sell three or four times as many paperback books in order to make a profit at the lower price. How can so many *unfamiliar* paperback titles be sold—competing as they must with reprints of famous books—without the benefit both of advertising and the displays and helpful salesmen one finds in bookstores? And with a price so low and sales so unsure how can the publisher provide the author with a decent royalty, or his book with effective promotion?

These and other questions have made many old-line publishers—some of whom have large investments in their hard-cover inventories—very doubtful of Cohen's vision of the future. As of now, they point out, it would be impossible to launch profitably most serious new books in paperbacks alone. And they note that attempts to put out new books in both hard covers and paper have not been highly successful.

But Cohen is confident that distribution and production of the books will improve—that answers can be worked out. In not much longer than a decade, he thinks, "most if not all popular fiction will appear in higher priced paper covers."

> Something new will be devised [he wrote recently]. There will be a shake-up and a shaking out; staid and tired publishers will succumb or merge; new publishers will rise and new techniques of communicating cheaply will be explored. The demise of anything ineffective, cumbersome, and unprofitable can only be a boon—particularly when our ability to communicate is at stake.

Whatever the outcome of this controversy, it seems to me a healthy one because, in one way or another, it might lead to a wider and more profitable distribution of good books. In any case, it brings me to a final point: Publishing *can* be a bitter war between editors who love books and businessmen who love only money; but if you are lucky, it should not be.

If you could peer into the minds of the stockholders and senior partners who ultimately control publishing policy, you could probably make—as Hiram Haydn recently did—a rough division into three groups: (1) those who are willing to publish little more than "titillating rubbish" in order to clear a high and sure profit; (2) those who publish *only* books which meet their very high standards of taste—usually (although not inevitably) at considerable loss of their wealthy family's capital; and (3) that large group of publishers who like to think of themselves as practicing the honorable profession of profitably publishing decent books for a variety of audiences, including some work of real distinction.

You'll soon be aware of the jolly hypocrisy, the fat-mindedness and the belief-in-one's-own-bookjackets that can abound in the upper levels of the publishing business; but in fact while most of the leading publishers do publish for profit each year a number of books which they wouldn't boast about at parties, they are, to their credit, often willing to issue several books of poetry each year at a loss; to take long risks on writers they—or their senior editors—believe are talented; to put out books on public questions as a public service. I do not think that they publish enough poetry, enough difficult or daring fiction, enough dissenting opinion. With honorable exceptions, they and their stockholders are no more eager to take losses than most entrepreneurs, no more willing to be unpopular or risk prosecution than most educators or lawyers or other professionals. However, when unlikely books succeed they are pleased indeed. More would be published if ways could be found to sell them to more people.

As I've tried to suggest to you, the ways that now exist to diffuse books in this swiftly changing, rich, and increasingly educated society are laggard and far from ideal; the challenge to you now is not only to pursue excellence—although that is certainly the most exciting part of the publishing business—but to find better ways to give excellence a wider and more profitable chance to be known.

CHAPTER 14

Two Views of the Reviews

The correspondence that follows was prompted by Elizabeth Hardwick's article.

Dear Miss Hardwick,

Your article, "The Decline of Book Reviewing," startled me. I have pondered on the lonely situation of one, like yourself, who lives so apart from the common reader. In these circumstances your sympathy with the plight of the ordinary folk who read our national book-review media is surprising. You observe, in the process of warming up for your onslaught on the *New York Times Book Review* and its editor: "There come to mind all those high-school English teachers, those faithful librarians and booksellers, those trusting suburbanites, those bright young men and women in the provinces, all those who believe in the judgment of the *Times* and who need its direction." As one in the business of distributing books, I'm heartened by this concern of yours for the faithful, the trusting, and the (provincial) bright.

While most of my associates in publishing would agree with you in condemning critical toleration of second-rate writing, many of your observations indicate a basic lack of understanding of the function of editors of general book-review media.

To give an example, you imply that the *New York Times Book Review* might well model itself on the pattern of the *Times Literary Supplement* of London. But you overlook the difference between the audiences for these publications; the former is part of a newspaper with a circulation of over one and one-third millions, the latter is an independent periodical with a circulation of just over 45,000. Surely the editor's function cannot be similar in these two cases. The editor of the *New York Times Book Review* is bound to give his large audience news about books as well as critical comment. The same observation applies to the *New York Herald Tribune Book Review* and, to a lesser extent because of its smaller circulation, to the *Saturday Review.*

It strikes me that you tend to be wide-eyed about British reviewers. That many of them write sharply and well is apparent, but you seem unaware of the amount of literary logrolling and intrigue that goes on in London reviewing circles—to an extent unmatched in this country. And haven't you observed that reviews of important fiction in British newspapers are often so brief as to amount to little more than passing comments?

You do make a valid point when you say that in England the important books are reviewed by people of literary standing, but when you indicate that this is in sharp contrast to American practice, I cannot agree. Your observation, "We don't pick up the Sunday *Times* to find out what Mr. Smith [meaning the ordinary man] thinks of, for instance, *Dr. Zhivago*," strikes me as a literary snobbism that shows a bland detachment from what goes on. For it so happens that *Dr. Zhivago* was reviewed in the *Times* by Marc Slonim, a leading authority on Russian literature, and in the *Tribune* by Bertram D. Wolfe, a fine scholar who has devoted his life to the study of Russian political and literary affairs.

When you castigate book-review editors and reviewers, whose names you use so freely, you sometimes belittle them without bothering to let the reader in on your specific reasons for doing so. In the case of Orville Prescott, for example, you simply observe that he may be a casualty of speed. This hardly strikes me as penetrating criticism, unless you are suggesting that daily book reviewing, which the ordinary book reader finds so useful, be discontinued.

Why are you so relatively kind about the effort made by *Harper's* and other general magazines to review current books? You do remark on the "often awkward and variable results" and intimate that this observation applies to the whole content of such magazines; but your really enthusiastic contempt is reserved for the national book-review media. What you fail to realize is that if the editor of the *New York Times Book Review* ignored the news value of books and failed to provide coverage, especially in the non-fiction field, his newspaper supplement would go out of existence and with it the opportunity to print literary criticism which reaches a very large audience.

Sincerely yours,
Cass Canfield
Chairman of the Executive Committee
Harper & Brothers, New York, N. Y.

To the Editors:

I am not much stirred by Mr. Canfield's reassurances and my own feelings of disaffection continue unabated. There appears to be a certain eagerness on Mr. Canfield's part to dissociate himself from disloyal opinion and a readiness to imply that he carries the common reader along with him. I have no doubt he does. I see no special reason at the present time to trust the common reader, the common publisher, or the common book-reviewing publications.

However, in reply to the letter. First of all, I discussed only the *Times, Tribune,* and *Saturday Review* because they are almost entirely read for their book reviews. Other magazines publish reviews incidentally or, in some cases, importantly, but they are not exclusively offered to public attention upon the strength of their reviews. I feel reviewing is the function of the three publications I discussed in my article. Mr. Canfield, on the other hand, sometimes seems to suggest that they are in some sense trade journals, giving out news and information about the publishing business and offering reviews as a bonus. He is more quick to explain their defects than to insist upon their virtues. But I think the *Times,* for instance, means to publish book reviews. I doubt that the bland, relaxed product is a matter of policy, necessary because of wide circulation. Wide circulation has not inhibited the seriousness of news reporting and comment, for instance. More likely, the superficiality and dullness are things that have just happened. Like the softness of middle age that appears, stays on until it seems natural—and no one minds so long as we feel all right.

I am aware of the limitations of English book reviewers. They are often pallid and over-refined. And I confess myself fascinated by accusations of intrigue and logrolling among the reviewers and editors. If this exists, perhaps it is the natural struggle for power where something of importance to society is at stake. Our own amiability does not give me the impression of high morality. Instead it is like the polite, impersonal stare of a cashier who takes in the money without being much affected in her private life by whether the bill is large or small.

Elizabeth Hardwick
Boston, Mass.

The Writer's Task

Bernard Malamud

It seems to me that [the writer's] most important task, no matter what the current theory of man, or his prevailing mood, is to recapture his image as human being as each of us in his secret heart knows it to be, and as history and literature have from the beginning revealed it. At the same time the writer must imagine a better world for men the while he shows us, in all its ugliness and beauty, the possibilities of this. In recreating the humanity of man, in reality his greatness, he will, among other things, hold up the mirror to the mystery of him, in which poetry and possibility live, though he has endlessly betrayed them. In a sense, the writer in his art, without directly stating it—though he may preach, his work must not—must remind man that he has, in his human striving, invented nothing less than freedom; and if he will devoutly remember this, he will understand the best way to preserve it, and his own highest value.

I've had something such as this in mind, as I wrote, however imperfectly, my sad and comic tales.

—Address by the Fiction Winner,
National Book Awards,
New York City, March 1959.

Novel Writing as a Career

MERLE MILLER

In general, novel-writing as a career is just about as secure as betting on the horses. There is always the short story, of course, but whereas ten years ago magazines printed 70 per cent fiction as against 30 per cent non-fiction, the ratio is now exactly reversed. F. Scott Fitzgerald used to be paid $4,000 for every short story accepted by the Saturday Evening Post. Today the fees paid for short stories are, in general, considerably less.

Most young writers who might have become good, steady pros for the slick magazines prefer television. The standards are about the same, and the market is greater. . . . Book reviewing? Well, yes; there is always that, and the New York Times Book Review pays a decent fee, but a magazine like the Saturday Review pays $35 for a thousand words, the same fee a journeyman carpenter gets for an eight-hour day. True, the carpenter does not get a free book.

At the other end of the scale, there is the movie industry, which now sometimes is willing to hire a writer for an occasional picture without insisting on a five-year contract with options. Somebody is alleged to have asked indignantly at a recent meeting of the Writers' Guild of America, West, "Do you realize there are writers right here in Hollywood who only make $250 a week?"

There are very few of those; a thousand dollars a week and up is not at all unusual, and a short stay in Beverly Hills to write a scenario can sometimes finance a long stay in New York to write a novel. A lot of people never get back to New York, though; the climate out there is wonderful.

In the United States today there are about fifteen thousand professional writers; that means people who at one time or another have sold something they have written, maybe only a four-line poem written for their local newspaper for a $2.50 fee. Of these fifteen thousand anywhere from twelve to twenty are able to make a living functioning solely as novelists; the rest must pursue some perhaps less satisfying but more profitable writing activity. Or else take a job.

—Authors Guild Bulletin, February 1957.

Notes on Contributors

KINGSLEY AMIS was an English novelist, poet, critic, and teacher. He wrote more than twenty novels, six volumes of poetry, a memoir, various short stories, radio, and television scripts, along with works of social and literary criticism. Amis's first novel, *Lucky Jim,* was published to great acclaim, translated into twenty languages, and won him the Somerset Maugham Award for fiction.

VANCE BOURJAILY was an American novelist, playwright, journalist, creative writing teacher, and essayist. He authored several critically acclaimed novels, including *The End of My Life, The Violated,* and *Brill Among the Ruins,* which was nominated for a National Book Award in 1970 and was praised in the *New York Times Book Review.*

ROBERT BRUSTEIN is an American theatrical critic, producer, playwright, writer, and educator who, in 1966, founded the Yale Repertory Theatre and served as dean of the Yale School of Drama. A former professor of dramatic literature, he now comments on politics for the Huffington Post. Brustein is a senior research fellow at Harvard University and a distinguished scholar in residence at Suffolk University in Boston. He was elected to the American Academy of Arts and Letters and in 2002 was inducted into the American Theatre Hall of Fame.

JOHN FISCHER was editor in chief of *Harper's Magazine.*

Mason W. Gross was an American television personality and academic who served as president of Rutgers University from 1959 to 1971.

Elizabeth Hardwick was an American literary critic, novelist, and short story writer. She authored three novels: *The Ghostly Lover*, *The Simple Truth*, and *Sleepless Nights*. She was a professor at Barnard College, a fellow of the American Academy of Arts and Sciences, and helped establish *The New York Review of Books*,

Alfred Kazin was a writer and literary critic who authored many works, including *On Native Grounds: An Interpretation of Modern American Prose Literature*, *A Walker in the City*, and *New York Jew*. In 1996 he was awarded the first Truman Capote Lifetime Achievement Award in Literary Criticism.

Stanley Kunitz was a Pulitzer Prize-winning poet who served as the United States Poet Laureat and as the State Poet of New York. Kunitz received many honors, including a National Medal of Arts, the National Book Award for Poetry, the Bollingen Prize for a lifetime achievement in poetry, the Robert Frost Medal, and Harvard's Centennial Medal.

Archibald Macleish was an American poet and writer awarded three Pulitzer Prizes for his work. MacLeish served as the Boylston Professor of Rhetoric and Oratory at Harvard University. He held this position until his retirement in 1962. From 1963 to 1967 he was the John Woodruff Simpson Lecturer at Amherst College.

Budd Schulberg was an American screenwriter, television producer, novelist and sports writer. He was known for his 1941 novel *What Makes Sammy Run?*, his 1947 novel *The Harder They Fall*, his 1954 Academy Award-winning screenplay for *On the Waterfront*, and his 1957 screenplay for *A Face in the Crowd*.

ROBERT B. SILVERS was an editorial board member for *Harper's Magazine* and served as editor of *The New York Review of Books* from 1963 to 2017. Silvers's awards and honorary degrees include the National Book Foundation's Literarian Award, the American Academy of Arts and Letters' Award for Distinguished Service to the Arts, and the Ivan Sandrof Award for Lifetime Achievement in Publishing. Among other honors, he was a chevalier of the French Légion d'honneur and a member of the French l'ordre national du Mérite. He was awarded the 2012 National Humanities Medal by President Barack Obama.

C. P. SNOW was a novelist and English physical chemist who also served in several important positions in the British Civil Service and briefly in the UK government. He is best known for his series of novels known collectively as *Strangers and Brothers*.

FRANK YERBY was a popular American writer who wrote a total of 33 novels and is best known for *Dahomean* and his 1946 historical novel *The Foxes of Harrow*, which was the first novel written by an African-American to become a best seller. In 2006, Yerby was posthumously inducted into the Georgia Writers Hall of Fame.

Printed in the United States
By Bookmasters